Studio Glassmaking

Studio Glassmaking

RAY FLAVELL & CLAUDE SMALE

VNR VAN NOSTRAND REINHOLD COMPANY
New York Cincinnati Toronto London Melbourne

Library of Congress Catalog Card Number 79-39889
ISBN 0 442 30021 2

Designed by Rod Josey

This book is filmset in Garamond and printed
in Great Britain by BAS Printers Limited,
Wallop, Hampshire, and bound by
Webb, Son & Company Limited at
Ferndale, Glamorgan

Published by Van Nostrand Reinhold Company Inc.
450 West 33rd Street, New York, N.Y. 10001
and Van Nostrand Reinhold Company Ltd.,
Egginton House, 25–28 Buckingham Gate, London SW1E 6LQ

Contents

Acknowledgements

The authors acknowledge their gratitude to:

West Surrey College of Art and Design which
provided the opportunity for us to start glassmaking, and to its Photography Service
Department (J. Moss and J. Malecki) for some of
the excellent photographs

Alaric Perry, who assisted so much in the
glass workshop

their families for their forbearance

Antony Atha, Esther Jagger and John Wallace
of Van Nostrand Reinhold.

Introduction

Woods, metals and clays have been worked successfully for many years by artists and craftsmen and these materials have also been the mainstay of traditional craft education in schools. Work in glass has been significantly absent. In schools, glassworking has barely existed, if at all, outside the chemistry laboratory where, from time to time, various glass components for scientific apparatus were made up.

Perhaps it was considered too dangerous; more likely, no expertise and no small scale equipment suitable for school or studio use was available. The situation seems to have been partly remedied, though only relatively recently, with the development of small tank-furnaces suitable for limited scale work. Such furnaces are nowadays available commercially in both the U.S.A. and the U.K., but it is very easy to build one. With the proliferation in recent years of these small furnaces, many artists and craftsmen are now adopting the medium, though few of these 'non-industrial' glassmakers were specifically trained in glasswork. Indeed, as facilities for training were virtually non-existent, there was little opportunity outside industry. Most practitioners are artists and craftsmen who have adopted glass as a medium later in their careers.

Thus there is a significant lack of a modern tradition in glassmaking outside the industry. As this is itself craft-based, there are those who would argue, perhaps with some justification, that there is no place for the 'studio worker' outside of 'industry'. But, by comparison, studio potters and metal workers have established a position not only in the galleries but in commerce as well, where they have set new criteria which the industry has tried to follow. Maybe, in time, studio glassmakers will fulfil a similar role.

Glassworking is already well established in further education and seems likely to make its way into schools to take up its rightful position alongside the traditional craft materials. This is bound to be a slow process because teachers themselves have to be taught, and above all convinced that, in the middle to upper schools at any rate, it is perfectly feasible to carry out glassmaking projects. It can be well done: it can be badly done. Much will depend on the goodwill of the industry to give the assistance and encouragement that is so badly needed. Hopefully, the industry will no longer tolerate the insignificant position of glass in the fields of education and craftwork and will be keen to ensure that facilities for study develop along the right lines. It is important also that 'industry' and the 'studio glassmaker' come to terms with each other. Aims must be clarified and preconceptions and fears dispelled so that no mistrust can arise, for misunderstanding is a great impediment to progress.

The authors hope that this book will be of some assistance to those who wish to become involved with glass.

Advice on technique is given where appropriate to assist the novice in the initial stages, though in glassmaking no set rules apply. As such, the book will, it is hoped, help others to avoid many pitfalls and be of practical help in learning skills and techniques which the trained professional carries out intuitively.

Safety

There is no denying that, when used indiscriminately or carelessly, glass can be highly dangerous. When cold it breaks into fragments which can cause severe lacerations, and when hot it can cause burns. These are the obvious hazards. Surprisingly, accidents seem few and far between, probably because we are all well aware of the dangers of broken glass and handle it with extreme caution. Likewise hot glass wins our respect. If commonsense precautions are taken, the workspace properly laid out and sensible procedures followed, the risk is minimised.

Always remember that glass on cooling is subject to stress, and sudden thermal shock can cause thick pieces to disintegrate with great force. Discarded pieces should be returned immediately to a proper cullet-bin, made of metal, where they can shatter safely. The bin should be lidded to prevent contamination by foreign bodies.

Blowing irons and punties should also be returned to a bin immediately after use so that residual glass, cooling on the ends, can break off safely.

CAUTION:
Glass remnants break from the pipe easily if immersed in water and this is common practice, but the thumb *must* be kept over the end or boiling water may flow out and cause scalding.

Any glass fragments (normally called cullet) retrieved can be returned to the furnace in due course.

Glassmaking is a fascinating spectacle and will attract onlookers. The workshop should be made safe for such people who are liable to touch or pick things up without knowing the dangers.

The workshop should be arranged so that tools and materials are conveniently at hand where they are needed. The metal (molten glass) will not wait whilst the glassmaker hunts for tools, and burns are more likely to occur if he has to stretch or move from his normal operating position. Forearm sleeves made of a non-combustible material with elastic ends offer some protection.

Many of the materials used in batch making are poisonous – lead and arsenic oxides particularly. Also, during the melting process noxious fumes are given off and an extractor hood is essential. For these reasons, schools are strongly advised to work from cullet and not to attempt their own batches. The use of lead in schools is in any case forbidden. The glassmaker who wishes to make his own batches should treat all materials as if they were toxic and should wear protective clothing and masks. The novice may well suffer some discomfort from the heat and glare of the furnace and it is advised that some form of shield be arranged for protection.

Chapter 1

What is Glass?

General Characteristics

To the layman, glass is a hard, transparent, brittle material which fractures easily into lethal fragments – dangerous stuff! To the glassmaker it is a material possessed of a wider range of properties, many of which he has come to know through working it in the molten state.

When cold, it is harder than most metals and resistant to abrasion. In scientific terms it is almost perfectly elastic; a suitable section when bent out of shape will recover its original form almost exactly when released. It is an excellent insulator for heat and electricity. Its broken fragments are sharp and dangerous because it has no regular internal crystal structure presenting 'natural' cleavage planes; it exhibits what scientists call a conchoidal fracture, much exploited in the working of obsidian implements by ancient man.

Glasses can be highly transparent, passing a high proportion of light rays. Their remarkable refractive qualities have been exploited in glass cutting for centuries, the variously angled planes reflecting, absorbing or dispersing light like so many prisms.

When heated, glasses take on a different set of characteristics. They do not have a sudden melting point; as the temperature is raised, viscosity decreases. Thus, in its working range, a glass may have a consistency ranging from 'syrup' to 'thick toffee'. Most glasses are extremely ductile and may be drawn into the finest of fibres for the manufacture of glass-cloth. Theoretically, a lump of glass which could be

Fig. 1. Quartz crystals from Cornwall. Photo: Geological Museum.

held in the hand could be drawn into a single fibre hundreds of miles long.

Some glasses occur naturally. Highly siliceous lava cools to form natural glasses such as obsidian. Pumice is a form of 'foamed glass' caused by the liberation of gases during the cooling of lava. When sand is struck by lightning a glass called 'fulgurite' is produced.

The Structure of Glass

Chemical compounds tend to divide into two groups, those which are crystalline and those which are amorphous. Most materials are crystalline. This means that when they solidify on cooling from the molten state or from precipitation, a molecular structure is developed which has a regular geometric pattern. These crystal structures may take a variety of forms: for instance some, like common salt, are cubic; some are prism shaped; and some take the form of octahedra. The outer shape of the crystal reflects the arrangement of the atoms making up the molecule. The three-dimensional system of bonding of the crystal structure serves to locate each molecule in relation to its neighbour and, as they cannot move, the material must possess the rigid properties of a solid.

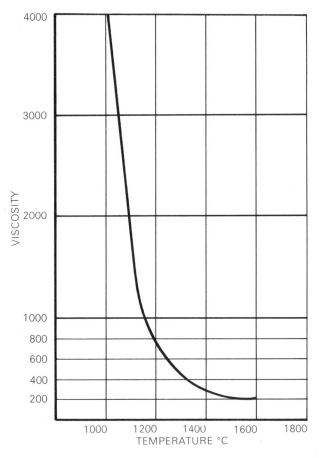

Fig. 2. Typical temperature/viscosity graph.

When a material is in a molten condition or in solution no such regular molecular arrangement exists, and the material is then called amorphous. The molecules of a liquid are linked by weaker bonds in a mainly random pattern. As the liquid moves, these bonds are constantly breaking and reforming in different arrangements. The viscosity of a liquid, or its resistance to flow, is an inverse measure of the readiness with which such rearrangements take place. All liquids can be considered to have some viscosity and this invariably increases as temperature is lowered.

Glass structure is amorphous. It is in all respects a liquid, exhibiting for the scientist the characteristics of a liquid which is exceptional in one respect alone: its viscosity is so high that at low temperatures its fluid properties can only be measured on a vastly expanded time scale. When hot it flows fairly easily, but when cooled its rate of flow is very much reduced. Fig. 2 shows how viscosity decreases with temperature rise.

Glass in the state in which we handle it in everyday life can be described as a 'rigid liquid', though it presents many of the physical characteristics of materials which are normally considered solids. Even at ambient temperatures it is still on the move, though a change in shape could only be measured over thousands of millions of years. The following table illustrates a comparison of times for a given degree of deformation to take place at various temperatures.

Temp. °C	Time
965	1 second
742	30 seconds
660	1 minute
538	1 hour
427	1 day
316	1 year
254	1000 years
Room temperature	35,000,000,000 years

For most liquids there is a temperature at which, on cooling from the molten state, crystallisation takes place: the material undergoes a change of state from liquid into solid – the familiar process of freezing. Water, it is well known, freezes into ice without difficulty and fairly rapidly at $0°$ C. Materials like water which are very fluid in the molten state form into crystals quickly. This is because the process of freezing entails the rearrangement of molecules and in the less viscous liquids they can move fairly easily. In the more viscous liquids there is greater internal 'friction' which makes it less easy for the molecules to move.

Glasses are made up of silicates and when these are molten they are still highly viscous. For this reason 'freezing' or crystal formation is spread over a wide temperature range and does not occur at a clearly defined point as in the case of water. If the glass is cooled far below normal crystallisation temperatures, the viscosity becomes so high that the internal molecular rearrangements cannot take place. In this case, the molecules become 'locked' in their random or amorphous arrangement so that the resultant solid possesses the characteristics of a 'congealed liquid'.

Glass, then, can be thought of as a liquid which has been cooled past its theoretical freezing point and is too cold and stiff to freeze.

It is of course possible to cool molten glass in such a way that it becomes crystalline and, if crystals do form on cooling, a glass is said to be 'devitrified'. For all glasses there is a temperature range within which this can happen, and recipes have to be devised to minimise this tendency. The upper temperature of the range, known as the 'liquidus' temperature, defines the point at which crystals begin to appear on cooling or begin to dissolve on heating. Above the liquidus temperature, glass cannot devitrify. Devitrified glass possesses some of the characteristics of a vitreous ceramic material such as porcelain, and has been employed for making pestles and mortars.

Scientists are still not entirely clear on the exact nature of glass; they assume that in the solid state it is much the same as the liquid and often describe it as a 'supercooled liquid'. It is a mutual solution of a number of substances which cannot be described by a simple formula. The main glass-forming compounds are oxides of silicon, boron and phosphorus. These all have the ability to form with oxygen in a chemical pattern which produces a tetrahedron-like system of molecular bonds.

How Glass is made

The main component of glass is silica, but silica alone cannot be used for glassmaking. To melt silica, temperatures of over $1700°$ C are required – high enough to fuse the refractories of many furnaces! The melting point of the silica must somehow be reduced to practical limits, and in common glass this is achieved by adding fluxing agents which produce a mixture possessing a melting point lower than that possessed by either substance separately. The most common additives are soda, lime and potash – the alkaline earths. When about 25% of soda ash (Na_2CO_3) is added to silica, the melting point is reduced from $1700°$ C to $800°$ C. Unfortunately, the resultant material cannot be used for glassmaking because it is sodium silicate ($NaSiO_3$) or water-glass, which is soluble in water. To obtain a non-soluble glass it is necessary to include a stabiliser, commonly limestone ($CaCO_3$). Thus a typical common glass might have a recipe:

Sand	(SiO_2)	65%
Soda ash	(Na_2CO_3)	20%
Limestone	($CaCO_3$)	15%

When preparing a batch, raw materials to these proportions are fired in a furnace to over $1500°$ C, the temperature required to make the batch being much higher than that required to maintain the glass in a molten state in the furnace. For this reason, it is common practice to include about 20% of cullet (broken up scrap glass) to assist the initial fusion.

Ideally, glass must be as fluid as possible in the furnace so that 'fining' or 'plaining' can take place. This is the process of removing from the glass all the many small bubbles which tend to remain in suspension, and it usually consists of introducing agents which produce larger bubbles. These, because of their greater buoyancy, flow upwards more quickly and in so doing collect and carry with them the small bubbles. In olden days, wet wood was pushed to the bottom of the mass. This produced many bubbles and left little residue.

The viscosity of a glass is generally matched to its working requirements. Those glasses which undergo a protracted manufacturing process must possess a long viscosity range. Glass for blowing must remain stable on the iron yet sufficiently workable to allow the various forming operations to be carried out. Viscosity may be reduced by adding soda, boric oxide or potash, and increased by adding silica and alumina.

Softening temperatures for common glasses are between 400–800° C. Boric oxide, phosphoric oxide, lead oxide and potash all lower the softening temperature.

The Raw Materials

SILICA

Silica is found on the earth in greater abundance than any other material. It is estimated that, in all its forms, it accounts for some 60% by weight of the earth. The next most common material is alumina which takes up 18%. These two substances are the basic materials of the ceramic and glass industries.

Silica occurs naturally in a variety of crystalline forms and for almost every type there is a specific industrial application which can make use of its special characteristics. Sand, quartz, cristobalite, flint, agate, opal and sandstone are all forms of silica. Apart from its pure form, silica is also found in combination with other materials such as alumina. Most of the silica used for glassmaking comes from quartz in the form of sand. Following the decomposition of original rock under the action of weathering agents, quartz crystals are washed downstream by rivers until the rate of flow of the water is too slow to keep them in suspension. Then they are redeposited to form sand beds. Sandstone rocks derive from sand beds which were deposited in this way in primeval times. Not all sands are suitable for glassmaking on account of the impurities they contain. Ideally they should be 99% pure silica. Iron oxide is a common impurity, and if present in even the smallest quantities has the effect of staining the glass green.

SODA

Soda is added to the mix to form sodium silicate and, as this is a soluble material, a stabilising component such as lime is essential. Soda is a strong flux and a high soda content produces a glass which melts easily, is soft and can be blown to shape with ease. The viscosity range can be extended by increasing the soda content.

POTASH

Potassium compounds, like soda compounds, are strong fluxes but, weight for weight, potash is less effective than soda. When potash is used, the metal is generally more viscous and takes longer to melt. Potash based glass is harder than soda glass, but it is frequently used with lead oxides to produce a bright glass which is soft enough to cut easily.

LIME

Lime is a powerful flux and reacts with silica at very low temperatures to form calcium silicate which is the essential stabiliser. Increasing the lime content increases viscosity and the rate of melting, though at high temperatures lime-rich glasses can be less viscous than soda-rich glasses. Increased lime also leads to more rapid stiffening on cooling. Without lime, glasses have a runny consistency and are difficult to work. Barium oxide and magnesia act similarly.

LEAD

Lead oxide is a very powerful flux, mostly added in the form of red lead (Pb_3O_4) or less frequently in the form of litharge (PbO). When present, it reduces viscosity and considerably reduces the viscosity range. The resultant glass is softer and so can be cut more easily than lime glasses even though it is more brilliant. When used with potash the effect is particularly brilliant, and the combination lead/potash is the basis of cut glass and best tableware glass. 'English crystal' is a lead/potash based glass having a typical recipe of $\frac{1}{3}$ lead oxide, $\frac{1}{2}$ silica and the remainder potash.

The Various types of Glasses

Glass serves a multitude of purposes and its chemical composition can be varied to impart special qualities to match specific applications. Cooking utensils, for instance, have to withstand constant thermal shock; windscreens must not break up into dangerous fragments; and optical glass must meet its own stringent specifications. There are infinite ways of compounding glasses with shades of difference between them, but the three broad divisions are:
Soda/lime/silica
Lead crystal
Borosilicate

SODA/LIME/SILICA GLASS

This, the most common form of glass, has already been described. Because the materials are plentiful and the manufacturing processes fairly simple, the glass is cheap to produce. It tends to have a greenish tinge due to traces of iron oxide. It is used for bottles and containers, windows, domestic ware, light bulbs, glassfibre, building blocks etc.

LEAD CRYSTAL

This glass is composed of silica, lead oxide and potash. Quite large quantities of lead can be added. It is easy to cut and engrave, it looks brilliant and has a large working viscosity range. Mainly it is used for best quality tableware, and cut glass.

BOROSILICATE

Borosilicate glass is made by a fusion of silica and boric oxide. The latter was first introduced as a constituent by Michael Faraday. Its essential characteristic is its low rate of thermal expansion and contraction, hence it is highly resistant to thermal shock and is universally used in any application where the glass is subjected to heat stress, for example, ovenware. 'Pyrex' is a well known brand name.

Apart from these three main types of glass there are many specialised glasses, the most outstanding of these being silica glass.

SILICA GLASS

Silica glass is made from almost 100% pure quartz silica and although its chemical composition is simple it is extremely hard to manufacture. The melting point, being over 1700° C, demands special furnaces and even when the silica is melted it is so highly viscous that fining is difficult. However, once it has been made, it possesses outstanding qualities of heat resistance and transparency.

Glass and Pottery Glazes

The glassworker and the potter both work with silica, but the potter will mostly work with silica combined with aluminium oxide in the form of clay or glaze. Clay is an aluminium silicate having a typical formula $Al_2O_3\ 2SiO_2\ 2H_2O$ – a combination of alumina, silica and water. Glazes are composed of similar materials but in different proportions.

The glassblower forms his pieces quickly; once he has begun the making process the material stays in the viscous state for a relatively short time only. The potter is involved with a lengthier process; he coats his clay with a layer of powdered glaze and must place it in a kiln to attain the temperature at which the powder fuses into an even coating. This firing cycle must necessarily be slow because it is governed by the rate at which the clay body can be heated and cooled. If a clay pot were covered with common glass powder the 'glaze' so formed would run down the sides of the pot like treacle before the firing was complete. Something is needed to stiffen the glaze so that, although it fuses, it remains in place on the pot. This is the function of the alumina content, though it also assists in matching the coefficient of expansion of the glaze to that of the clay body. Thus potters' glazes contain, in addition to silica, up to 20% of alumina whilst glasses, except in special circumstances, contain not more than about 1%. By varying the proportions of silica and alumina (plus some additional fluxes and colouring agents), the potter is able to regulate the properties of his glaze.

Table 1
TYPICAL BATCHES FOR VARIOUS TYPES OF GLASSES

	SODA/LIME/SILICA				LEAD CRYSTAL		BOROSILICATE
	Glass Fibre	Bottles	Windows	Domestic	Full Crystal	Semi-Crystal	Domestic
SAND	55	72·3	73·0	71·02	55·64	64·3	80·3
ALUMINA	14	1·0	1·00	3·0			2·5
SODA	0·5	15·5	12·0	16·5			4·7
POTASH			0·3	1·05	11·03	19·2	
LIME	21	11·05	10·0	5·4		9·6	
BORAX	8·5						12·5
MAGNESIA			3·3	3·0			
MANGANESE DIOXIDE						0·5	
IRON OXIDE		0·15	0·1	0·03	0·03		
SULPHUR TRIOXIDE			0·3				
LEAD OXIDE					33·3	6·4	

Chapter 2

Glass and Colour

Making the Glass Clear

Iron compounds in various forms are present as impurities in most earth materials, and glassmaking materials are no exception. The smallest trace of iron oxide is enough to produce a distinct greenish tinge and, whilst this may not be visible in thin sections, it is very pronounced where glass is thick. For cheap bottle glasses or for glasses which will be coloured, an iron-bearing sand may be selected for the colour it gives. Iron compounds may also enter into the melt from the furnace refractories or from the ends of the blowing irons. It is not possible to remove the iron, so if clear glass is required the green colour must be disguised. Iron oxide may be present as either ferrous oxide (FeO) or ferric oxide (Fe_2O_3). (Notice that ferric oxide Fe_2O_3 contains a higher proportion of oxygen atoms than ferrous oxide FeO. When a material changes state by gaining oxygen, the process is described as 'oxidising'; when it loses oxygen the process is described as 'reducing'.) Ferrous oxide imparts a blue-green cast to glass, ferric oxide imparts a yellowish colour. The blue-green tinge of the former is more easily visible than the latter and, for this reason, when ferrous oxide is present in a glass it is usual to convert it to the ferric state so that it is less obtrusive. This can be achieved by adding oxidising agents, typically arsenious oxide, potassium nitrate (saltpetre) or sodium nitrate. These release oxygen into the melt, which keeps any iron oxide present in the pale or ferric condition. (In addition, oxidising agents combine with any organic materials which may be present, counteract any reducing tendencies of the furnace gases, and prevent the reduction of substances which might otherwise easily be reduced. Any gas bubbles released assist a little in the fining process.)

The process of changing colour by oxidation is known as chemical decolourisation. Additionally, decolourisation may be carried out by a physical process, in which a stain is added to the glass which is complementary to its natural colour. (Two colours are said to be complementary when, between them, they absorb to an equal extent the rays making up white light.) The effect of the added complementary colour is to 'correct' the natural colour so that the glass appears clear. Actually, the glass is always somewhat less clear because a proportion of the light rays throughout the spectrum have been taken away. A suitable added colour to 'balance' the greenish tinge of iron is purple, a colour produced by manganese oxide. In an average batch, from 100–250 gms of manganese dioxide would be added to one kg to act as a decolourant. Manganese oxide also acts as an oxidising agent, assisting in the conversion of ferrous iron oxide to the yellow ferric state.

Colouring the Glass

The apparent 'colour' of glasses may not be due to added colourants. The sense of colour we get when we observe glass may derive from the way in which light rays have been affected. Light which falls on glass is partly transmitted or refracted and partly absorbed. As the refractive index varies from glass to glass, different parts of the spectrum may be affected. Thus glasses may appear to have a natural 'colour'. There are two main ways of imparting colour to glass:

1. Colloidal dispersion
2. Staining with metallic oxides.

COLLOIDAL DISPERSIONS

A colloidal dispersion consists of minute particles of material distributed in a liquid in such a way that they are not properly dissolved, and therefore do not become a solution, yet are not merely in suspension. Thus they never settle out on standing and can only be filtered off with the finest of meshes. When light passes through a colloidal dispersion the particles scatter the light rays: some are stopped, others pass through and, since some of the rays of the spectrum are subtracted, the light which is observed appears coloured. The effect is well illustrated in fog which, as is well known, absorbs blue light but allows red light to penetrate.

The materials which are generally included in glass to give this effect are the metals gold, silver and copper, and the non-metals selenium and sulphur.

STAINING GLASS WITH METALLIC OXIDES

It is possible to add various oxides to the batch so that the glass is self-coloured but, as glass is highly viscous, it is not easy to distribute the pigment in the batch. It is usual to disperse the powder thoroughly in a small batch which is then added to the main batch.

Metallic oxides are the essential colouring agents. A few of these are volatile and some, because they are unstable at high temperatures, are likely to change colour as they change their chemical state. For example the most stable form of iron oxide, and a common colouring agent, is red iron oxide, Fe_2O_3, but in the furnace this may well turn to the green form FeO. Notice that one atom has been taken away: it has been taken up by the hydrocarbons in the fuel to support combustion. This is known as a reduction process and is easily instigated by starving the furnace of oxygen. The reverse process, oxidation, can be carried out in an oxidising flame. In this case the metallic oxide changes colour because it gains oxygen. The effect is well illustrated in ancient oriental ceramic glazes; the turquoise celadons of the Sung period and the yellower colours of the Yüeh period all derive from the red form of iron oxide. Metallic oxides are also greatly affected by the fluxes present in the mix, particularly if they are lead or

alkaline-based. Many such colours depend upon a reaction with a basic glass material.

Red

Most red coloured oxides are unstable at high temperature and cannot be used for staining.

Rich ruby coloured glasses are made by colloidal dispersions. Gold chloride, obtained by dissolving the metal in hydrochloric and nitric acids, when added to the batch in the smallest quantities (0·001%), produces a rich ruby colour. When the glass is first worked, a straw colour is obtained, and the glass must be reheated to a dull red heat to develop the true ruby colour. Overheating produces a purple/brown colour.

Precipitates of cadmium, selenium and sulphur act in a similar way and produce glasses which are clear and bright.

Copper colloids also produce a rich red which is mostly used for flashing clear glass.

Yellow

When iron oxide and manganese dioxide are added to a batch in the right proportions an amber tint results. The manganese dioxide, being a strong oxidising agent, reacts with the iron to produce the ferric yellow colour. As has previously been described, small amounts of these materials, carefully balanced, will make a batch clear. By varying the proportions and increasing the quantities, a range of colours from bright yellow to orange and green can be produced.

Silver chloride can be used but more usually it is used to stain the surface after forming has been completed.

Cadmium sulphide produces a bright yellow.

Pure sulphur makes a good yellow colour except in lead glasses when it reacts with the lead to form lead sulphide.

Carbon compounds assist the formation of yellow.

Blue

Cobalt oxides have been used for centuries to stain glasses blue. The technique was well known to the ancient Persian and Syrian glassmakers.

Cobalt oxide is extremely potent, 0·001% producing a strong bright colour. On its own, cobalt gives a 'raw' blue and it is usually tempered with iron or manganese.

Early glassmakers used to burn raw cobalt ores to obtain a crude oxide which they called Zaffre.

Violet stains are obtained by a combination of nickel and manganese.

Green

Chromic oxides withstand high temperatures and are used for green stains, though the colour produced has a yellowish tinge. By comparison, cupric salts give a greenish blue.

Nickel compounds are sometimes employed, though the colours obtained from these vary with the composition of the glass. In potash glass purple is produced, in soda glass blue/brown, and in lead glass, red.

Black

Black glass is produced by adding large quantities of manganese tempered by additions of copper, cobalt or iron.

Purple

Manganese dioxide produces a purple stain and in excess quantities gives brown. With lime/potash glass it produces a turquoise colour and with lead/lime/soda glasses it produces a red colour.

OPALS

Opalescence is produced in glasses which contain two phases having different refractive indices. There are two main types: emulsion opal (phosphate) and crystalline opal (fluoride).

Emulsion opals

An emulsion is a mixture of two immiscible liquids, one being finely dispersed in the other.

Phosphates are added to produce a phosphate glass which becomes dispersed in the silica glass. At lower temperatures the two glasses 'separate', but if the temperature is raised the two phases become miscible and a clear glass results. Thus, if phosphate glass is rapidly heated and cooled, the resultant glass will be clear, but if this is reheated and held at a temperature just above its melting point, the opal effect will appear. As the effect is due to the suspension of transparent droplets in a transparent material there is little loss of light – the rays are merely deflected.

Crystalline opals

Crystalline opals are similarly produced by the precipitation of a crystalline phase within the glass. A suitable fluoride glass will precipitate crystals of calcium and aluminium fluorides.

Chapter 3

Historical Techniques

Fig. 3. Amphora, moulded on a core, 3 in. high, in opaque white glass decorated with manganese purple. Egyptian, 3rd to 4th century B.C. Photo: Pilkington Bros. Ltd.

The Egyptians

Nowadays glass is so commonplace that we take it for granted, and it is all too easy to forget the intricacies of its manufacture and the achievements of early glassmakers who worked with such primitive equipment.

Scholars cannot say exactly how it was that glass was first made, but the earliest evidence of a form of glass seems to date from about 4000 B.C. when a turquoise glaze was applied to small clay ornaments. Such jewellery was made in quantities and exported widely, but whilst pottery glazes were fairly common, it was not until 1500 B.C. that artifacts were made entirely of glass. Even then the first objects, or the known ones at least, were made for items of personal adornment or for the embellishment of the chattels of the rich. Relics of the tomb of Tutankhamun reveal glass fragments inlaid alongside precious stones, and it must be supposed that glass was considered a very precious material.

The furnaces of the period must indeed have been crude, and it is thought that the preparation of the glass, or 'metal' as it is called, involved several firings, the core from each being ground to a powder before reheating. But despite such limitations, the Egyptians managed to make hollow ware by an unusual technique of winding molten glass on a core.

CORED GLASS*

A form corresponding to the inside shape of the required vessel was turned or otherwise modelled on the end of a metal rod. It is thought that the material used for the form was either ferruginous clay containing organic material (dung?) which on burning away left an open texture, or sand bound together by a clay slurry. In either case the cores were probably limewashed. When the shape was centred and dried thoroughly, molten threads of glass were drawn and wound round the core until a suitable thickness had built up. The process was slow and the work had to be constantly reheated. A common decorative adaptation was the winding on of threads of different colours and, by drawing a metal pin across the windings, each colour was drawn into the next to produce a 'feathered' effect more commonly seen on traditional English slipware and some forms of cake-icing. The piece was finally heated to fuse the windings together and, on cooling, the metal rod contracted and was easily withdrawn. Then the sand/clay

* See *The Egyptian Sand Core Technique* by Dominic Labino. Reprinted from the *Journal of Glass Studies*, Vol. VIII, 1966, and available from Corning Glass Museum and Pilkington Glass Museum.

Fig. 4. Persian bowl, 4 in. diameter, with cut facets. 5th century A.D. Photo: Pilkington Bros. Ltd.

Fig. 5. Roman cameo, white glass over manganese purple. 4th century A.D. Photo: Pilkington Bros. Ltd.

core, being a friable mixture, was easily broken up and knocked out of the interior. Unavoidably, the inside surface took on the rough impression of the sand core.

Egyptian glasses were commonly coloured turquoise and yellow, and tin oxide was not unknown as an opacifier. A considerable industry seems to have centred on Alexandria whose products were widely distributed by Phoenician traders.

Roman Glass

Egyptian workers and methods were imported and an industry was established in Rome itself. The first recorded use of window glass dates from this period. There is some evidence to suggest that early glass-makers used glass in the manner of the lapidary; many surviving pieces show evidence of considerable grinding on the wheel. The famous Portland Vase was made by this technique, a layer of translucent white glass being fused on to a dark base glass and the cameo shapes developed by grinding away the top white layer to expose the dark ground.

A development of the sand core technique involved laying up fragments of different coloured glasses over a core. These, when heated, fused together to produce a vessel with a mosaic-like effect.

GLASSBLOWING

Whilst scholars cannot say exactly when or where glassblowing was first carried out, it is certain that the earliest known examples date from the 1st century A.D., the technique no doubt made feasible by improvements in furnace building. The introduction of the blow pipe was a highly significant event in history, comparable with the invention of the potter's wheel, for the fact that hollow-ware could now be quickly and easily made meant that glass immediately became a competitor with metal and clay. Early forms suggest that they were blown inside clay moulds. From the 1st century onwards, glass was a common article of trade and was generally

19

Fig. 6. Syrian vase, 4 in. high, in pale green glass with blue trailed ornament. 4th to 5th century A.D. City of Liverpool Museums.

available for the storage of wines, perfumes and medicaments as well as for tableware.

In the later Roman period cut glass, engraved glass, millefiori and enamelled wares were not uncommon; indeed by the fall of the empire, there was mastery over all of the basic processes as we know them today. In Europe, little was made to surpass Roman ware until Renaissance times. In the Near East, however, enamelled ware, lustres and engraving were developed to a high art. It is recorded that in the 6th century clear and coloured glass was fitted to the windows of Santa Sophia in Constantinople, a practice which was to spread across Europe.

Venice

Glassmaking had been carried on in Venice since the 11th century, but not until the 13th century did its products become well known. The main industry was located on the island of Murano because, it is suggested, flames from the furnaces could not set fire to dwellings in the city, and because the secrets of the industry could be closely guarded. (Guild systems were set up to assist in this and to look after the interests of the glassmakers. Whilst the glassmakers enjoyed high status and social privileges, they were harshly dealt with if they broke their code of conduct.)

Venetian glass was soda/lime based, the alkali being obtained from burnt seaweed and plants, and the silica from pebbles of natural quartz. Quite early on the Venetians had rediscovered the art of decolourising glass with manganese and their glass became renowned for its water-white clarity. Sometimes clear glass was textured by plunging it into water when hot and immediately reheating. This produced an ice-like appearance. Sometimes glass fragments were rolled into the molten glass and fused on to the surface. Enamel painting was common, much work being heavily over-ornamented. The famous mirror industry continued until the 19th century.

LATTICINIO AND MILLEFIORI

These techniques were not unknown to the Romans but they were developed to a high art by the Venetians in the mid-18th century.

Latticinio

Rods of coloured or opaque glass were arranged around the sides of a near cylindrical former which held them in place whilst they were taken up on a gather of molten glass. When reheated, the rods fused with the gather to become coloured or opaque stripes

Fig. 7. Plate, 8 in. diameter, decorated with opposing white spiral threads – a reticello. Made in Murano, 16th century. City of Liverpool Museums. (Opposite).

22

Fig. 8. *Covered ceremonial goblet 14 in. high, the cover with a plain knopped finial. Possibly Murano, late 16th century. City of Liverpool Museums. (Opposite).*

Fig. 9. *Wine glass decorated with spiked gadrooning with a thread circuit. Attached to the hollow stem are a pair of yellow 'ears' with six pinched lobes. Murano or Façon de Venise, early 17th century. City of Liverpool Museums.*

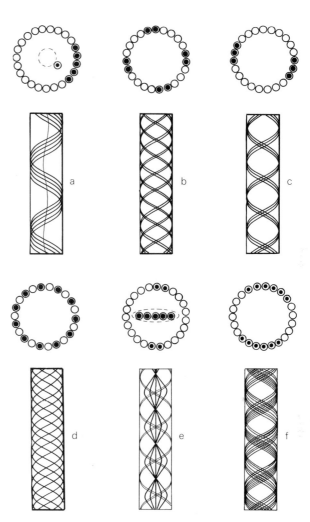

Fig. 10. *The latticinio technique.*

in the mass and this, when drawn out and twisted, produced the spiral decoration commonly seen in the stems of glasses. Sometimes the drawn-out glass, or cane as it is called, was chopped into lengths, put back in the cylindrical former and taken up on another gather. Thus vessels could be made with a

23

Fig. 11a. *Heating cane in a supporting cylinder for latticinio.*

Fig. 11b. *Collecting the cane on the blowing iron.*

Fig. 12. *Decoration of a form by latticinio technique: a. cane arranged in cylinder; b. cane gathered on parison; c. marvering in; d. cutting off with parrot nosed shears brings canes to a point; e. the resultant blown shape.*

Fig. 13. *Paperweight, French, mid-19th century. Perhaps Saint Louis. Photo: Victoria and Albert Museum. (Opposite).*

delicate tracery of lace-like patterns. Fig. 10 illustrates how different spirals could be achieved by varying the arrangement of the canes. In (a) a single cane is attached to a small gather which is then enclosed in a larger one before insertion in the cylinder. The central twist seen in (e) is achieved by making the gather around a flattened cylinder or sleeve of glass containing the cane. Fig. 12 shows the technique used for the decoration of a form.

Millefiori

The term millefiori means 'thousand flowers' and the

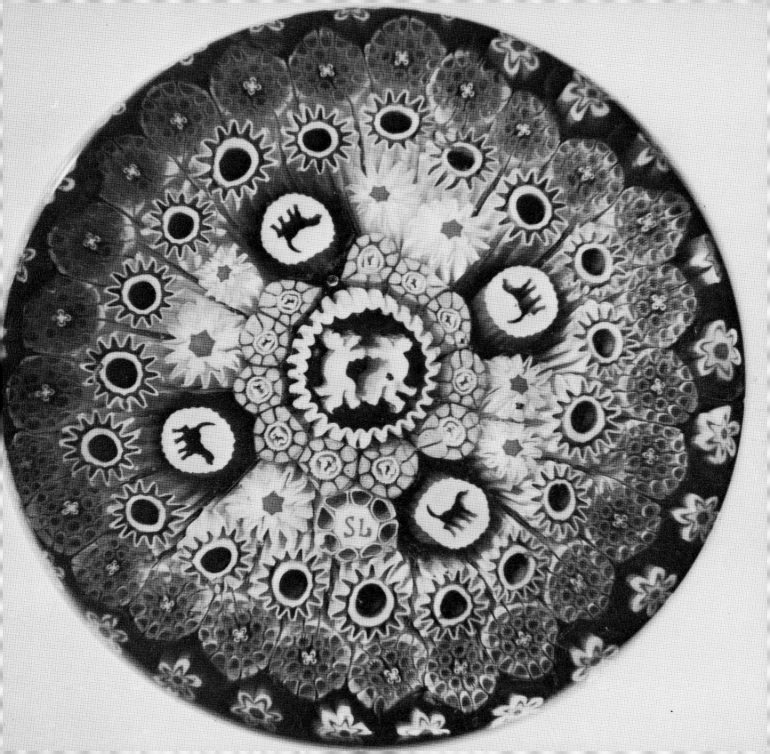

technique was not unknown to the Egyptians in 1400 B.C. Lumps of coloured glass were placed together and heated until they fused. The resultant mass was then drawn into long canes whose sections retained perfectly, though in reduced scale, the pattern of the original arrangement. The process was not dissimilar to that used for the production of seaside rock. From the canes, sectional discs were cut, sometimes obliquely: these were arranged together and fused into the form of the required piece.

More recently, decorative cane was produced on the glassblower's iron. A small first gather was marvered into a regular section and a second gather in a different colour made as a coating to this. After marvering, the whole was in turn coated with a different colour and so on. Simple regular sections were made by pressing on the marver; more complex sections – star shapes etc. – were made in a mould. The mass was drawn into cane by a pontil attached to the end. By repeating the process, cane of infinite variety of section was produced and, in later years, the millefiori technique was thoroughly exploited in the making of paperweights. To make these, coloured cane was cut to short lengths and arranged in a simple iron mould shaped like a flat ring which served to hold the pieces in place. It was not unusual for upwards of a hundred sections to be incorporated. The whole assembly was then heated, taken up on a punty and coated with successive gathers of crystal glass until its final shape was achieved.

In later years, Venetian craftsmen moved to other countries – England, France, Spain and Germany, a significant works being set up at Antwerp.

Bohemian Glass

The first Bohemian glassworks were small affairs scattered over forest land where there was a plentiful

Fig. 14. German 'Waldglas'. A covered beaker 10 in. high in pale green glass. Early 16th century. Photo: Pilkington Bros. Ltd.

26

Fig. 15. Green glass roemer 6 in. high, the base encircled by a milled ring, and raspberry prunts on the stem. Dutch, about 1655.

supply of wood for fuel and wood-ash for fluxes. The glass produced was known as 'forest glass' or 'Wald-glas', a common 15th century form being an open vessel decorated with spots of applied glass. The typical 'roemer' had a foot which was formed by winding a thread of glass over a conical core of wood or metal. Whilst production techniques have changed – the original impressed spots or prunts are nowa-days moulded in – the form of the vessel remains un-changed to this day.

During the later Middle Ages carved natural quartz or rock crystal had been much valued by the upper classes, and many craftsmen were employed in working it, but since rock crystal is considerably harder than glass (almost as hard as diamond) and difficult to carve, it was extremely expensive. Bo-hemian glass showed so great an advance on earlier glasses and so closely resembled the prestigious rock crystal that it was much sought after. Just before 1700 it was made with a potash/lime content which not only imparted extra clarity but provided a suit-able metal for deep relief engraving. By the mid 1750s Bohemia had developed into a major centre for glassmaking. Furnaces were much improved and work was organised on an 'industrial' basis. Since it takes half a ton of wood to produce one pound of the crucial potash, flux manufacture was undertaken by specialists.

Glass in England

In A.D. 680, according to Bede, Benedict Biscop, Abbot of Wearmouth sent to Gaul for glaziers, but from about 1250 there is evidence of a native glass-making industry. Yet by the Middle Ages few houses were glazed. In 1575 a patent was granted to Jacopo Verzelini to make 'drynkyne glasses such as be accustomablie made in the town of Murano'. At

27

Fig. 16. Wine glass 6 in. high, the bowl set on a drum shaped knop decorated with raspberry prunts, and the stem with a single white twist. English, about 1760. Photo: Pilkington Bros. Ltd.

about this time wood was becoming scarce, and in 1615 there was a royal proclamation forbidding the glassmakers to use it.

The most significant contribution made by the English was the development of lead/flint glass, known as lead crystal. In the late 17th century the Glass Sellers' Company retained George Ravenscroft to research into 'a perticuler sort of Christaline Glass resembling Rock Christall'. Lead had been commonly used as a component in ceramic glazes but not in glasses. The lead crystal Ravenscroft developed not only possessed a brilliance which surpassed all previous glasses but was readily cut into facets on the glass cutter's wheel. It also led to significant developments in optics.

By the early 1800s glass pots and furnaces were much as we know them today, though by the middle of the century they were almost all coal burning.

Fig. 17. Glass furnace described by Agricola (1490–1555) in De Re Metallica, published in Basle in 1556.

Chapter 4

The Glassblowing Process

First Stages in Glassblowing

Glass which is formed by hand on a blowing iron is described as 'free blown' or, more usually, 'off hand'.

In the first part of this chapter, the basic steps are described for the benefit of the complete novice. Further processes are then described which can be carried out by those who have had some practice.

In industry, a single glassblower seldom makes a complete article. Each furnace pot is worked by a team of men, a special task being alloted to each man. One, the 'foot blower' or 'gatherer', collects the molten glass on the iron; a second, the servitor, may make the parison or add a foot; another may blow; and there is usually a 'boy' who is an apprentice to the team. The composition of the team may differ but invariably each team is supervised by a 'gaffer' or 'workman' who has overall responsibility for the work. He does the final shaping, attaches handles and forms lips. In England, the team is known as a 'chair', a term which clearly derives from the fact that a team of glassmakers serves one glassmaker's chair.

Before commencing glassblowing, the operator should always ensure that his workshop is well organised; that the floor is clear of unwanted rubbish and impedimenta which might cause him to trip; that his tools are at hand and properly prepared and that his work surfaces are clear. Apart from facilitating the making process, this reduces the risk of accidents.

Some common terms should first be explained. A 'gob' or a 'gather' is the blob of molten glass as it is first gathered on the iron. A 'parison' describes the gather after it has been trued and has received its first bubble of air. The glass material is commonly referred to as 'metal'. The various tools and pieces of equipment are described as they are met with in the text.

There are few basic operations in the art of glassblowing, but in this chapter these have been analysed and described stage by stage to assist the beginner over his initial difficulties. These stages have been selected for description only and should not necessarily be seen as separate operations. Successful glassblowing depends upon a steady rhythm of movement.

At the beginning it all seems very difficult, but passable skills are soon developed. When he has acquired some of the basic skills, the novice will soon evolve his own methods to improve technique. It should be remembered that the skills necessary to manipulate molten glass are unique; nowhere in the working of other materials is it possible to acquire experience which will be of any value whatsoever in handling the blow pipe.

RHYTHM AND CONTROL

Undoubtedly the greatest difficulty at all stages is keeping the molten metal under control and centred on the end of the pipe. To achieve this, the pipe must be constantly rotated – even when the various forming operations are taking place. The novice invariably finds difficulty in co-ordination and performs a series of violent manoeuvres in a desperate attempt to prevent the metal from falling off the end. His movements are corrective, often over-corrective, of droops in the glass which he seems unable to anticipate. Control, balance, timing and sensitivity toward the material have to be learnt and co-ordinated into steady rhythmic movements. No words can describe the necessary feeling for the material, how to match the operation to the viscosity of the glass, but sensitivity develops with practice and a rhythm of working becomes intuitive. Eventually the pipe is manipulated correctly with the utmost economy of movement, sufficient just to retain the glass in a symmetrical shape so that all movements simply preserve this state of equilibrium. Of course, all manipulations will be quicker when the glass is hot and straight from the furnace, but they become slower as the glass gets more viscous on cooling.

REHEATING

At regular intervals and at all stages of the glass-blowing process, the work will require reheating in the flame of the furnace. If the piece is allowed to cool too much, it will shatter under the influence of the cooling stresses set up. Over-cooling can also result in the work breaking from the pipe due to thermal shock when it is readmitted to the furnace. As a general guide, it is time to reheat the work when it begins to lose its yellow/orange colour in the thicker areas.

PREPARATION OF THE GLASS

Although the proportions of raw materials to make up a glass are described elsewhere, it is not always practical to melt these from the raw state in a tank type furnace. This would require a temperature considerably in excess of normal glassworking temperatures. A tank furnace is best filled with 'cullet'. This is broken up scrap glass which can be purchased from glass suppliers.

During the initial melting process, gases are liberated by the chemical reactions taking place and whilst the agitation of the mass caused by the escaping gases assists thorough mixing, it also unfortunately leaves small bubbles in suspension in the molten mass. These are often known as 'seeds' and have to be cleared before the glass can be worked. In time, they will rise up and clear under their own buoyancy but the process can be accelerated by raising the temperature of the furnace, thereby reducing the viscosity of the glass and allowing the bubbles to flow more freely. When heating cullet, bubbles are less of a problem, but even so it is advisable to wait for a period of twenty-four hours

30   *Fig. 18. Reheating a piece in the flame from the burner.*

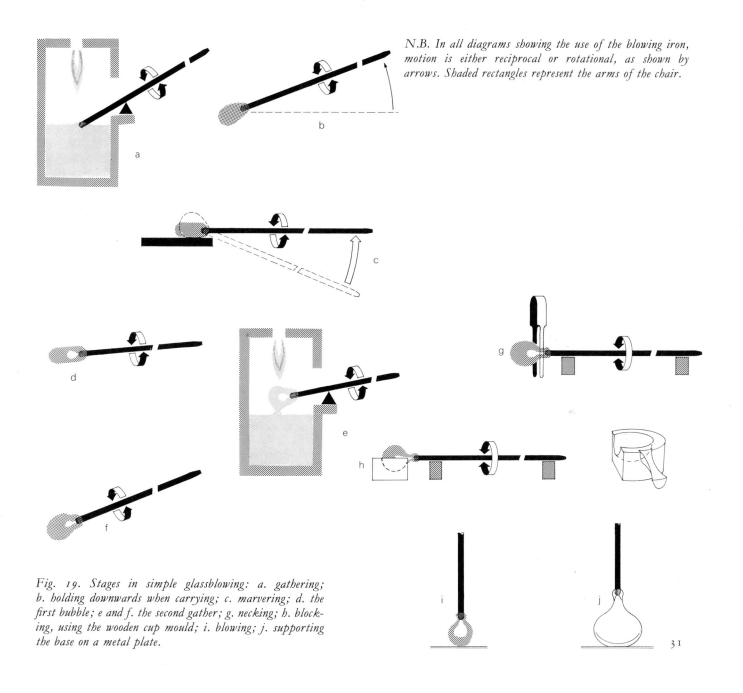

N.B. *In all diagrams showing the use of the blowing iron, motion is either reciprocal or rotational, as shown by arrows. Shaded rectangles represent the arms of the chair.*

Fig. 19. Stages in simple glassblowing: a. gathering; b. holding downwards when carrying; c. marvering; d. the first bubble; e and f. the second gather; g. necking; h. blocking, using the wooden cup mould; i. blowing; j. supporting the base on a metal plate.

31

to allow the glass to clear. This is known as 'fining'.

WORK WITH THE BLOW PIPE

The blowing iron is a strong iron tube about 5 ft. long, $\frac{3}{4}$ in. in diameter and with a bore of about $\frac{1}{4}$ in. The end or 'nose' at which the glass is gathered is thicker and the mouthpiece is usually tapered. See Fig. 73.

Before the 'nose' of the pipe is introduced into the molten glass it should be preheated in the mouth of the furnace. If it is too cold, the glass will not adhere properly and it will so chill the glass that it may not be possible to blow the initial bubble. It should not get red hot, however, or a scale will form from the iron and contaminate the glass. 'Cronite' tipped irons are available which obviate scaling. Most working holes are fitted with a metal rest to support the irons whilst they are heating.

THE FIRST GATHER

The end of the pipe is laid on the glass surface, not completely submerged, and gently rotated. Then by carefully raising it and pulling back slightly (Fig. 20.), a gather is collected. Initially it is not advisable to wholly immerse the nose of the pipe; if the metal enters the end it becomes difficult to blow. Some practice is required to gather the 'right' amount of material in the 'right' way but it is a critical part of the blowing operation. The aim should be to gather 'off the end' of the pipe rather than to wind it round the end. If the gather is not even, it will be difficult to keep a symmetrical shape in the operations to follow. The novice will at first suffer some discomfort from the intense heat of the working hole, but with practice the gather will be quickly made and less time spent in the exposed position. On withdrawal from the furnace, the gather will be found to have the consistency of thick treacle and only constant rotation of the pipe will prevent it running off. It is best to carry the pipe horizontally or pointing slightly downwards. If it is held upwards the glass tends to run back down the pipe, when for the next operation, marvering, it is required 'off the end'.

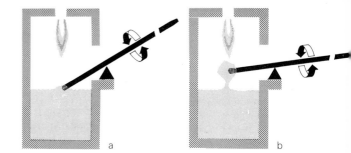

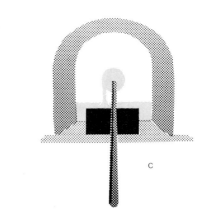

Fig. 20. Stages in making a gather.

MARVERING

(Fig. 21.) The marver is a substantial flat bed, usually metal, about 2 ft. 6 in. × 1 ft. 6 in., with a prepared surface (see Fig. 76). Any material which withstands the temperature of the glass is suitable. Marvering consists of rolling the gather to and fro on this plate to make the shape regular and symmetrical. The initial rolling movement should be quite slow and should be quickened only when the glass has assumed a basically cylindrical shape. Steady gentle pressure is required. The glass will not crack during this operation; as it is straight from the furnace it is too hot for cooling stresses to be introduced. The aim and effect of marvering are:

1. To reduce the thickness of material around the nose of the iron.

2. To bring the glass into a controlled shape *beyond the end of the pipe.*

3. To chill the surface of the molten glass. This chilling makes the outer skin more viscous.

To coax the glass beyond the end of the nose, the iron should be slowly raised as in Fig. 19c. Alternatively, the nose can be rolled on the back edge of the marver whilst gently pulling on the iron. The shape of the gather can be adjusted by altering the angle of the iron to the marver but this should be done gradually, in time with the rolling movement, or the glass will run off centre. Normally, marvering is car-

Fig. 21. Marvering.

ried out at about $1000°$ C, but large gathers are easier to marver if they are allowed to cool and stiffen.

THE FIRST BLOW

(Fig. 19d.) A sharp puff is now given to the end of the pipe and, almost simultaneously, the thumb is slipped over the open end. The retained pressure causes a small bubble to appear after a few seconds in the inner part of the glass. The pressure of the bubble is contained by the outer viscous skin. There is a knack to this operation which the beginner may take some time to acquire and, to start with, he may prefer to sustain pressure by keeping the pipe in his mouth. With this method it is not easy to see when the bubble has formed in the glass, and a mirror placed at floor level and conveniently angled to reflect the bulb will be of great assistance. Contrary to common belief, at its proper working temperature little pressure is required to blow glass. Once the air bubble has been introduced, the glass is generally referred to as the 'parison'.

The skilled glassworker is usually able to collect the right amount of glass in one gather but the less experienced find it easier to build up the desired amount in a series of layers. The iron should be returned to the tank and the end once more dipped in, when a fresh layer will readily adhere. Obviously, the larger the piece intended, the more gathers have to be made. Second gathers cannot be made until the gather already on the iron has cooled and stiffened somewhat.

THE CHAIR

The majority of forming operations are carried out on the glassworker's chair (see Fig. 72) and it is at this point in the sequence of operations that it is brought into use for the first time. The chair provides two arms or supports at a convenient height, along which the pipe can be rolled with a to and fro action. This removes the weight of the pipe from the arms of the operator and provides a steady, even means of controlling rotation. The operator is thus able to devote

33

Fig. 22. The second gather.

comes to 'crack off' the piece from the pipe. It is achieved very simply by rotating the neck of the bulb between the arms of tongs held under steady pressure. The necking must of course be done beyond the end of the pipe.

BLOCKING

(Fig. 19h.) Following the second gather, the work may again be marvered or the glass may be blocked or shaped by a wooden cup mould. This consists of a hemispherical shape, excavated in a piece of beech or fruit wood, with a handle attached (see Fig. 23). It is used when working in the chair as in Fig. 19h. As the parison is rotated on the arms of the chair, the mould is allowed to travel with it. The parison thus rotates

Fig. 23. Blocking.

all his attention to the job in hand. In all operations it is essential to retain a symmetrical shape and it is usual before rotating the iron on the chair to turn the iron slowly and in such a way that the glass falls on centre.

Having centred the work the first operation to be carried out is 'necking'.

NECKING

(Fig. 19g.) The purpose of necking is to reduce the thickness of glass at the break off point so that the fracture can occur in the right place when the time

with the mould and is formed into a symmetrical shape. The action can best be described as caressing; little force is required. The mould is stored in water and used wet. The inside becomes charred to a layer of soft carbon and this, when presented to the surface of the glass, has a polishing effect. As the outer layer of glass becomes chilled, the effect is similar to marvering. Blocking moulds may be truly spherical or tapered for making conical shapes.

PREPARING THE PARISON FOR BLOWING

Before the parison can be blown it must be prepared so that it will inflate into the desired shape. Adjustments will have to be made to the size of the bubble, its position, the thickness of the glass around the bubble and the overall shape of the parison. Experience is the best guide to the form that a parison will produce, but obviously a spherical parison will produce a spherical form and an elongated parison an

Fig. 24. Adjusting the shape of the parison.

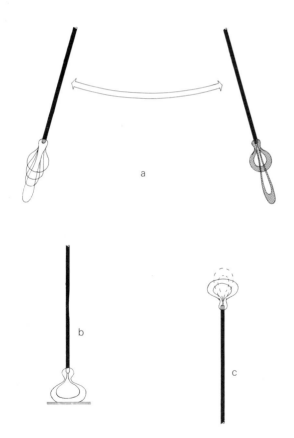

elongated form. Unless the bubble itself is properly centred within the parison there will be variation in the thickness of the glass surrounding it, and when the glass is inflated the thin part will inflate more easily than the thick part, so that an eccentric form is produced. The marver can be used to adjust the thickness of the glass and to direct it to the top, middle or bottom of the parison as desired. A flat parison can be made by lowering on to the marver, as in Fig. 24b. An elongated parison can be reduced to a more squat shape by holding it vertically, as in Fig. 24c. By swinging the iron, as in Fig. 24a, centrifugal force can be used to elongate the parison and to direct the glass to its base.

BLOWING

When the parison is satisfactorily prepared, blowing can commence. Professionals usually do this with the pipe at an angle of nearly 45 degrees and resting on one arm of the chair, thus enabling the blower to correct any deformations by rotating the pipe. The novice, however, will almost certainly find this position difficult. It is not easy to blow and turn the pipe at the same time and an easier method is to stand on a raised platform allowing the pipe to fall vertically clear of the floor. This way the glass is less likely to fall off centre, but it will tend to droop and elongate. The novice will almost certainly prefer this method and will allow for some elongation when preparing the parison. If the blown shape elongates too much, the base can be lightly supported on a metal plate on the floor as in Fig. 19j. This will result in the base becoming flattened, but this is in any case an alternative method for 'flatting the base'. The novice will learn by experience to relate the timing of the blowing to the temperature; if the glass is too hot the form will be limp, but if the thumb is closed over the end of the pipe, air is enclosed and the form stabilised.

When the basic form has been blown, it is likely to be near pear shaped and it can now be adjusted to what the maker desires. The sides and the base can

35

a   b

Fig. 25a and b. Blowing with the iron hanging vertically.

be flattened with the paddle or, if an elongated form is required, it can be swung in an arc on the pipe. It can be made more regularly cylindrical by rolling evenly on the marver, or it can be waisted with wooden ended tongs. There is no set way of manipulating the form; each blower devises his own methods and is ready to make adjustments as the glass dictates. Neither is there a standard set of tools or method of using them.

It is at this stage that, in his eagerness to put the final touches to his shape, the novice often forgets to reheat the work, particularly the area near the nose of the pipe. This tends to cool by the time the blowing stage is reached and, if allowed to cool too much, the piece may fall off. Sometimes it is possible to wind

another collar of molten metal around the end of the pipe to keep it hot. (In the initial stages, the novice will wish to crack off his piece from the pipe at this stage so that he can repeat these basic movements.)

When the basic form has been established on the blowing iron, it is time to turn one's attention to the neck end which inevitably will be the thickest part. It is not possible to work it whilst it is on the iron so it must be transferred to a punty.

PUNTYING
(Fig. 26.) The punty is a straight iron rod whose name derives fron the French word 'pontil' – a bridging tool. The nose of the punty is pre-heated to below red heat and a very small gather made on the end.

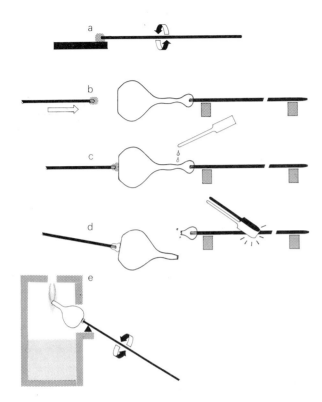

Fig. 26. Puntying: a. marvering small gather on punty; b. attaching to base; c and d. cracking off; e. reheating fractured end. (Above).

This is marvered into a small cylindrical shape and is then carefully attached, usually by a second person, to the centre base of the vessel. The neck is then cracked off leaving the vessel attached to the punty by a very small area of glass. The process is not easy; operator A must keep the base of the vessel hot in the working hole whilst operator B prepares the punty on the marver. The two pieces must come together at a

Fig. 27. The puntying process: a and b. preparing the small gather on the punty; c. attaching the punty; d and e. cracking off. (Continued overleaf).

37

d

e

attach and crack the piece off in the normal way.

An easier method for the novice is to set up a V shaped trough on a bench and to crack off into this so that the piece is well supported for attaching the punty. It is desirable that the punty attaches by as small an area as possible so as to minimise the blemish, and glassmakers have different tricks to achieve this. A common method is to indent a cross in the end so that the attachment is by four points only; other methods are to dip the end in sharp sand or chalk so that an imperfect joint is made, or to indent the middle of the gather on the corner of the marver.

The moves described so far are the basic ones which the novice must practise until he acquires some control. After that he will wish to explore more sophisticated possibilities, and the best method of learning is through trial and error. Glassmakers devise their own methods and the descriptions of techniques which follow are included not so much in the expectation that they will be closely followed, but in the hope that they will serve to stimulate further experiment.

Annealing

In common with many materials, glass contracts on cooling and, because it has very low thermal conductivity, the surface cools before the inside. This means that the surface material *contracts* before the inner material and thus gives rise to stresses and strains. Usually, if glass is allowed to cool in the open air these strains are sufficiently strong to cause the piece to shatter. To obviate this, glass is always placed in a heated oven or 'lehr' to cool slowly after it has been formed. The process is known as annealing and allows an even dissipation of the heat. A pottery kiln can be used for annealing in studio work.

The annealing time depends not only on the composition of the glass but also on its form. Thick glasses hold more heat than thin glasses – heat will

similar temperature or colour. If the metal of the gather is too hot the weight of the vessel will cause it to fall over, but if it is too cold the piece may fall off unexpectedly.

When attached to the punty, the vessel must be rotated carefully until the glass by which it is attached stiffens sufficiently to support it without bending. It is not impossible for the glass blower to punty without assistance, though the main difficulty lies in working two pieces at once. He must quickly prepare the gather on the punty before the blown glass form cools or droops on the iron. The iron can be laid across the arms of the chair so that he can move to the nose end of the iron with the prepared punty to therefore take a longer time to dissipate from thick glass, and the annealing time will be longer.

Different glasses have different annealing temperature ranges – for a soda glass, for instance, the range is typically from 500–650° C. Above the upper temperature, the glass is so soft that no strain is possible. If the annealing is done at the lower temperature the process will be very prolonged on account of the stiffness of the glass. If it is done at the higher temperature there is the risk that more stresses will be set up on cooling. Clearly as the glass is softer at the higher temperature strains are more easily released.

When it is formed, glass can be cooled rapidly to its upper annealing temperature where it must be held and then cooled very slowly to the lower annealing temperature. No hard and fast rules can be given regarding the rate of temperature drop or what the temperature/time co-ordinates should be. For general purposes a constant temperature drop of 10° C per hour is recommended. The greatest danger lies in the lower range, where rapid hardening of the glass takes place.

Much can be learned by trial and error about the annealing range of a glass and the time/temperature limits necessary for various thicknesses. For normal studio type work a potter's kiln, when allowed to cool slowly, gives approximately the right rate of heat loss and so can usefully double as a lehr.

TOUGHENED GLASS

The annealing process can be used to induce stresses and strains selectively so that glasses may be strengthened to withstand various loads. It is well known that normal flat glass breaks easily on impact. This is because it is weak in tension, and fractures easily from the surface.

Toughened glass is made by rapid cooling of the outer layers of glass so that they are in tension about the inner layer which, it follows, must be in compression. 'Toughening' is carried out by force-cooling the surfaces with cold air blast. Once it has

been toughened in this way, the glass will remain intact only so long as the delicate balance of forces is maintained. The slightest nick in the surface may provide the weak point which gives way under stress, and the glass will shatter. Car windscreens well illustrate the point.

COMMON FAULTS

All novices tend to make the same mistakes and find the same difficulties. Before proceeding further, therefore, it should be emphasised that:

– at the initial blow, care should be taken to restrain the effort as soon as the bubble has been seen to form. At this stage, the glass will easily over-inflate and form a thin section;

– if the pipe is not constantly rotated, the bubble may burst through (Fig. 28);

– it is necessary particularly to keep the parison on centre when making further gathers, or an uneven thickness will result;

– when reheating a piece, the punty or the iron should be rotated at an even rate to ensure that the heat is evenly distributed. If there are local hot spots, these will be softer and will inflate more easily and lead to deformation;

– care should be taken in heating the nose of the pipe where the glass is attached. The glass in this area is considerably chilled by the metal, and thermal shock may cause the piece to snap off.

Fig. 28. Effect of blowing an uncentred bubble.

39

More Advanced Techniques

When the piece has been transferred to the punty, the end which has been severed is generally narrow and thicker in section and can be reworked in various ways.

It must first be reheated in the hot part of the flame, when it is very easy to make it even narrower by drawing it out with the tongs whilst rotating it on the

Fig. 29. Stages in opening a form with tongs.

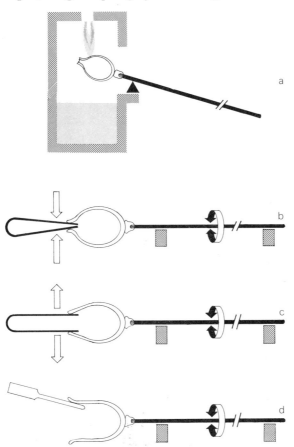

Fig. 30a and b. Drawing out with the tongs.

chair. More imaginatively, it can be cut with shears; folded back on itself; drawn out in the form of a crown; dragged back with a sharp point etc., etc. The worker will no doubt discover for himself a range of possible treatments. More orthodox treatments are described below.

MANIPULATING THE OPEN RIM

(Fig. 29.) If an open type of rim is required, it may be necessary first to remove some of the thicker material with shears. With the vessel attached to a punty, the neck is reheated in the hot part of the flame (a), and when suitably prepared the work is transferred to the chair. Pointed tongs are used to open up the neck whilst the vessel is rotated (b). It is usual to hold the tongs with the palm facing upwards. If they are allowed to open out gradually, the neck is stretched open (c). When the neck has thus been opened completely, it can be turned outwards to a bell shape by deflecting the tongs upwards (d). It should be noted that metal tools are more prone to leave marks than wooden ones. Fig. 31 illustrates from above the method of holding the tongs.

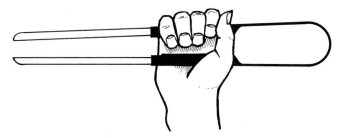

Fig. 31. Method of holding tongs to open a neck.

FORMING A BOWL OR PLATTER

(Fig. 32.) By opening the rim further with wooden tongs, a wide necked bowl or platter can be produced. Rapid rotation of the punty is necessary to spin the rim wide. The technique was commonly employed in earlier years to make window glass. The metal was spun until it flattened out completely. When cool, panes were cut from the disc. Glass made by this method was known as 'crown' glass.

Many of the tableware techniques – forming handles, spouts, stems etc. – require two operators and a fair degree of skill, and delicate stemmed ware cannot be made without a 'glory-hole' (see p. 82). The timing of each move with the correct state of both pieces of glass can be critical and, as some of the manipulations cannot be done quickly, much careful reheating of the work may be necessary. In any case, the heat capacity of thin walled pieces is low and if they cool too much they tend to shatter on reheating.

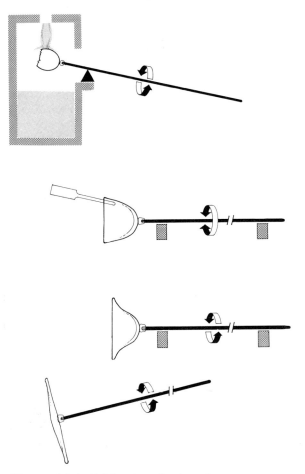

Fig. 32. Method of forming a bowl or platter.

MAKING A SIMPLE FOOT

The simplest method of making a flat base is to lower the form on to the marver or to flat it with a wooden paddle. The centre of the base may be pushed inwards to increase stability. Such a depression is known as a 'kick' and was commonly used on hand-made wine bottles.

Where a puntying or grinding stone is available, a

41

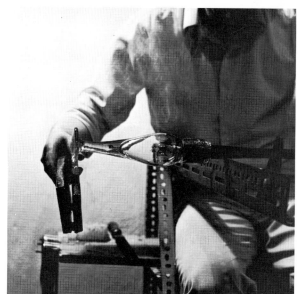

42

*Fig. 33a, b, c and d. Stages in making a vessel with a simple
foot.*

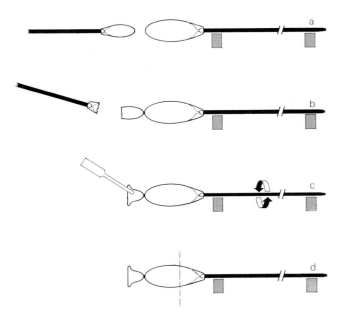

Fig. 34. Making a simple attached foot.

small concavity may be made in the base when the punty mark is removed.

The simplest form of applied foot (Fig. 34) involves two blowing irons, one carrying the main bowl form and the other the elongated foot form. The latter is attached and cracked off to form the foot, the foot rim being softened and smoothed by reheating. Any final bell shaping can be carried out at this stage and the whole piece finally puntied off.

STEMMED PIECES

(Fig. 35.) The bowl form is made and the iron tilted to a near vertical position as in (a). A second person makes a small gather and allows it to fall on the bowl. This is cut to length with shears (b). The stem so formed is adjusted and made symmetrical on the chair (c) and the piece is then inverted once again to the near vertical position. A blob from a second gather is deposited on the end of the stem (d) and

worked into a flat shape with a flattening tool (e). Any necessary shaping to the rim is carried out following reheating. The piece is puntied (f), cracked off (g), the rim trimmed with shears (h) and then fire polished before final cracking off and cooling in the lehr.

Fig. 35. Stages in making a stemmed piece. (Continued overleaf).

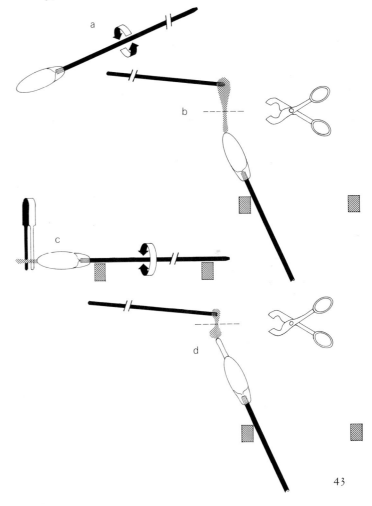

43

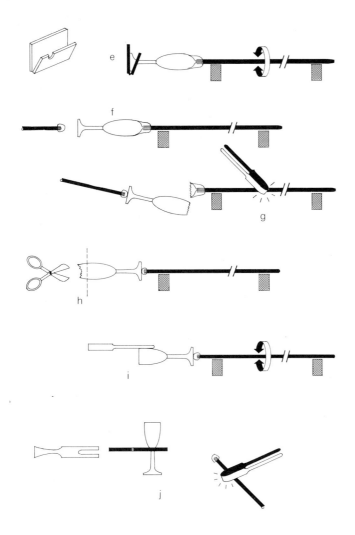

Fig. 36. The effect on form of ground finish or fire polish.

MAKING A HANDLE

(Figs. 37 and 38.) A shape is prepared and a second operator places a long gather on the side of the piece which is cut to length. The whole piece is then swiftly rotated one revolution to swing the handle outwards so that it is centralised and not pointing askew. This also has the effect of chilling it slightly so that it stiffens. By tipping the end of the pipe upwards, the handle is made to fall over, is assisted into shape and attached with a wooden tool. A lip can easily be worked by pulling out the rim with tongs or by making an indentation with a round piece of wood or brass tube.

LIDS AND KNOBS

These can be formed by methods already described. Knobs are best made by adding a small gather and working to shape with tongs. Flat lids can be spun.

COMPOSITE FORMS

It is possible to join glass shapes together in the hot state, but when large shapes are so joined very considerable skill is required to handle them on one iron. The novice is advised to make one main form to which are attached a series of smaller forms.

RODS AND TUBES

A gob is marvered to a cylindrical shape by the first

Alternatively, a parison can be made up with a thickness of glass at the base. This thick glass is necked and drawn out with tongs to form a stem, and a gather made on the end which is flattened into a foot with a flattening tool. The piece is then puntied and cracked off in the normal way. This method does not require a 'glory-hole'.

44

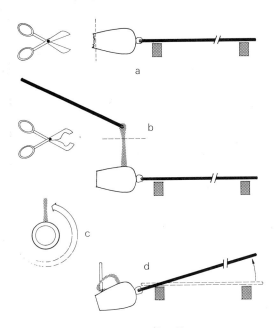

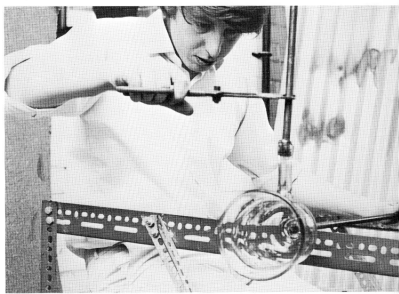

Fig. 37. *Method of attaching a handle.*

operator, and a small gather is made on a punty by a second operator and flattened to a disc shape. The cylindrical shape is reheated by the first operator and is then held upright over the flat disc so that the metal slowly droops until the end attaches to the disc. As soon as a proper join is made, the two operators walk apart drawing out the metal as they go. This, as it is stretched, is allowed to fall on a wooden board, and because of its thinness needs no annealing. The lumpy ends are cut off and later returned to the batch as cullet. Tubing is similarly made except that a hollow parison is made for drawing out.

Fig. 38. *Applying a handle: a. the punty is supported by the glassworker while the molten glass is attached; b. as the second operator withdraws the punty, the section of the glass thins and is cut off to length by the glassworker; c. as soon as the handle is severed, the piece is rotated (Overleaf); d. turning over and attaching the other end.*

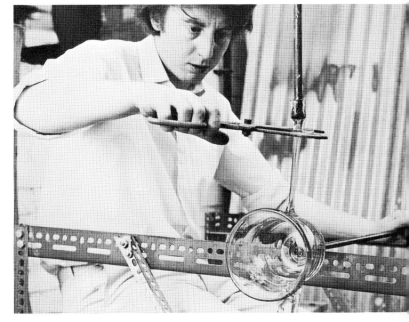

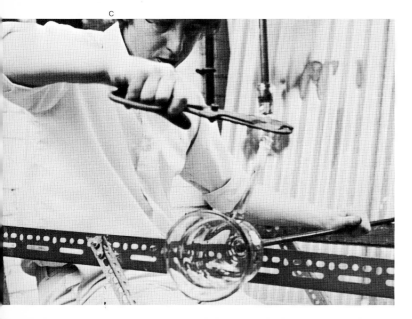

Trapping Air Bubbles

SIMPLE BUBBLES

A variety of internal shapes and effects can be achieved by trapping bubbles in the glass. A bubble may or may not be blown in the initial gather. The simplest method is to press a metal rod – the point of the tongs will do – into the glass so that it is thoroughly indented. A second gather is then made (rotating it rapidly so that it does not flow into the cavities) which forms a coating over the top, thus trapping air. If the indentations are made in a regular fashion, the bubbles will assume a regular arrangement inside the gob. If the gob is then blown, the bubbles will deform and flatten out into interesting shapes as the piece expands.

Fig. 39a, b and c. Stages in making air bubbles. (Below and opposite).

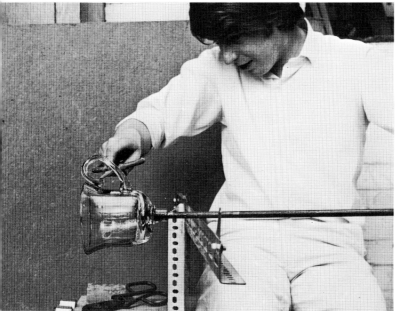

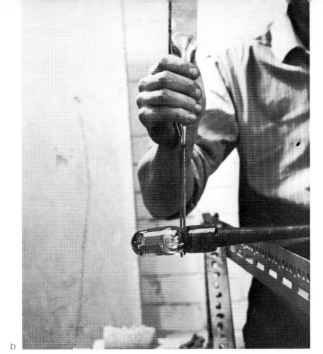

b

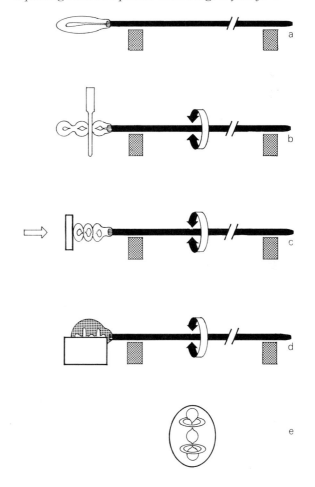

CIRCULAR BUBBLES

(Fig. 40.) An elongated parison is made containing a long regular bubble. This is necked with the tongs and compressed with the paddle so that the neckings close up to form deep recesses. A second gather is

Fig. 40. Making circular bubbles: a. parison with long bubble; b. necking with tongs breaks up a long bubble; c. pressing back with paddle; d. blocking; e. final form.

c

made which encases these recesses to form circular bubbles.

The usual practice in industry is to use a metal mould, generally one with honeycombed embossings on its inner surface. A gather is blown inside this and a second gather made over the top as previously described. Because the impression in the mould is geometrically regular, the bubbles so formed are also regular.

DECORATIVE EFFECTS WITH BUBBLES

If a bubble is made in a parison and the two sides impressed so that they join in the middle, they will adhere. If the piece is then reinflated, the join may be strong enough to prevent the piece assuming its original shape, so that a new form results. However if the area of contact is small the piece may more or less assume its original shape, but in so doing the join will be drawn out into a strand of glass crossing between the two sides. Clearly the area of contact will determine what will happen. If the sides are brought together so that they lightly touch in several places a piece with many strands joining the sides may be produced.

A Few Variations

A FORM WITH A 'SHOULDER'

(Fig. 41.) If a second gather is made on a thinnish bubble so that it only partly covers, the new gather will soften the original material and the uncoated part will remain stiff. Therefore when this is blown further a pear shaped form results. The process can be repeated to give more than one 'shoulder'.

GATHERING ON THE RIM

A gather can be made on the edge of the rim. This may tend to close up the opening and should in any case be trued with tongs. The thick edge so formed can be manipulated in a variety of ways: it can be pulled out and layered back on the side of the form or it can be extended to give a crenellated effect.

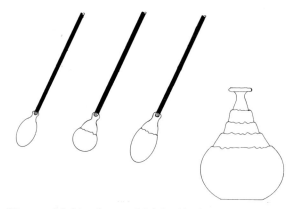

Fig. 41. Making forms with 'shoulders'.

ENCLOSED COLOURED FORMS

A small gather of coloured glass is attached to a gob of clear metal. The coloured glass is drawn out into shapes and manipulated into various forms. Over this, a second gather is made in clear metal to encase the whole.

LOCALISED COLOUR

Small discs of coloured glass cane are heated on a metal plate. A gather is prepared to pick these up. When the whole is reheated in the working hole and blown to shape, coloured areas will be formed in the vessel.

ENCLOSED TRAILS

Molten glass (which may be coloured) is trailed on to a prepared gather. This is encased in a second gather and blown to shape in the normal way.

Moulding Methods

SKELETON MOULDS

Skeleton moulds may be fabricated out of metal rod, sheet or wire and can be used for making forms which are recessed or indented. The process is illustrated in Figs. 79–82. As it touches only a small

a

b

Fig. 42a and b. Making a form in a simple skeleton mould of metal rods set in a metal block. (Left).

area of the mould, the glass tends to have few blemishes.

WOODEN MOULDS

Wooden moulds are not as durable as metal ones, though they will withstand up to 1000 impressions. Woods which leave a soft charcoal when burnt are most favoured; those which produce a hard charcoal tend to burn unevenly and leave an irregular surface. Wooden moulds are used wet and should be stored in water. Two-part moulds may be joined by a hinge but, for ease of operation, the hinge line should be some distance from the edge of the mould (Fig. 43).

METAL MOULDS

The metal moulds used in industry are generally made of cast iron but, for short runs, aluminium may be used. Schools possessing foundry facilities should have no difficulty making aluminium moulds.

Seam marks on finished pieces can be avoided by revolving the molten glass in the mould. This is achieved by rotating the blowing iron between the palms. If this method is used it is necessary to make a

Fig. 43. Hinged two-part wooden mould.

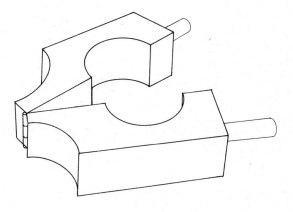

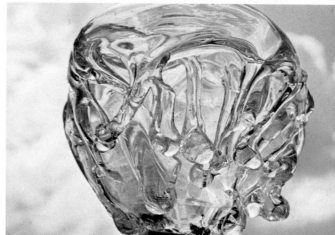

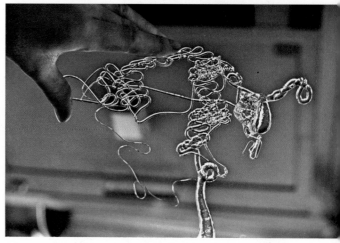

Left: drawing glass into a free form.

Top: a detail of the finished piece.

Above: the lace-like effect of this piece was achieved by trailing glass on the marver.

Opposite: decorative bottle with marvered-in colour. Ray Flavell.

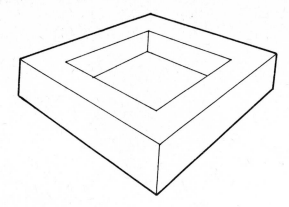

Fig. 44. Metal frame used on the marver to cast tile forms.

paste lining to the mould. The paste must be carbon forming, and is easily made from resin and linseed oil reduced to a viscous liquid. After application, the coating should be dusted with the finest wood dust and then hardened on in an oven at 80° C. A further layer should be applied and similarly dusted and then heated for about half a day at 70–80° C. Areas of moulds which may become sealed off should be vented so that steam can escape.

Often it is possible to improvise moulds by using discarded engineering components – especially castings containing hollow shapes. The Scandinavians have even produced ware made from snow and ice moulds. These have a crazing effect on the glass surface, known as 'crizzling'.

Chapter 5

Decoration

Hot Process Decoration

TRAILING FROM THE PUNTY

Molten glass can be trailed directly on to a form from a punty to make a relief decoration. More commonly, the form is rotated so that the trailed thread is wound on as a spiral, usually in a second colour. This is easiest to achieve if the blowing iron is held in a yoke which allows it to be continuously rotated in one place.

Much decorative work has been achieved by trailing shapes on to the marver. If threads are trailed around a parison they tend to act as bonds restraining the development of the form when it is blown, thus producing a constricted or waisted effect.

PRUNTS

A prunt is a blob of molten glass applied to a form for decorative purposes. The technique was very common on early European ware. When the glass is in a molten state it can easily be impressed with an embossed tool which, if made of metal, sufficiently chills the glass surface so that the relief does not flow out; the blob of glass is usually impressed immediately. A common form of prunt decoration is known as 'raspberry' on account of its resemblance to the fruit. Many 'found' objects with a suitable relief can be improvised. Wooden or plaster patterns will withstand small numbers of impressions.

EMBOSSING WITH A ROLLER

A wheel or roller with a decorated circumference can be rolled around a circular form or across a flat form to leave an impression. Suitable decorated discs can be made from wood or plaster and fitted to a bent wire handle.

COLOURED CANES

If canes of opaque glass are arranged around the inside of a cylinder, they can be picked up on a parison and melted in at the furnace mouth. These will appear in the final blown shape as bands of opaque glass.

The more ambitious may wish to experiment with 'latticinio' or 'millefiori' techniques, which are described in Chapter 3.

'CASING'

If vessels were made entirely of dark or highly coloured glasses, their thicker sections would be so

Fig. 45. Trailing a thread of molten glass from the punty.

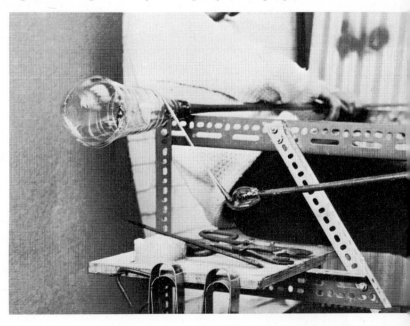

Making cane for latticinio.

Top left: a cast aluminium form supports the short pieces of white cane.

Middle: the cane has been picked up on a gather of clear glass, resoftened in the furnace, and is here being marvered.

Right: a punty is attached for drawing out the gather.

Below left: the second operator walks away with the punty and draws out the glass, while the glassmaker rotates the iron to produce a twist in the white threads.

Opposite: two goblets in cased amber. Ray Flavell.

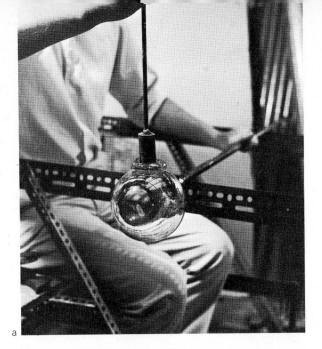

a

Fig. 46a and b. Stages in making a prunt.

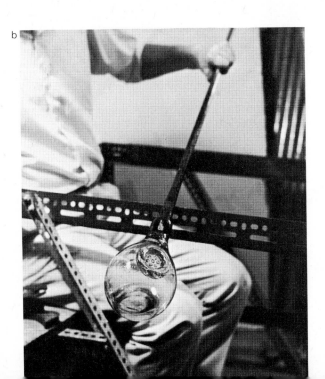

b

a

Fig. 47a. Cane to be heated is placed on a pan and held under the burner; b. when it has softened, it can be gathered on a punty or blowing iron.

b

dark as to be opaque. For this reason, clear glass is often 'cased' or coated with a layer of coloured glass which ensures all over consistency of colour. Sometimes the coloured layer is sandwiched between two layers of clear glass. Glass which has been 'cased' is commonly decorated by cutting or etching, the top layer being removed to provide a contrast with the under-layer. Elaborate pieces may be 'cased' in more than one colour, allowing multi-coloured patterns to be worked. The coefficients of expansion of glasses used when casing must match each other.

CASING FROM THE TANK

A gather of clear metal is taken on the iron and blown to a bulb, which is in turn rotated in molten coloured glass until an even coating is collected. Thus, when the piece is blown, it is coloured on the outside only (Fig. 48).

A 'half-cased' effect can be obtained by making a thick bulb in clear glass, flattening it at the base and attaching to its base a small gather of coloured glass. When reheated and blown, the piece will be coloured on its lower half only (Fig. 49).

VARYING THE INTENSITY OF COLOUR

(Fig. 50.) A bulb of clear glass is covered with a layer of coloured glass as previously described (a). Areas which are required to be lighter in colour are then impressed with a metal rod (b). This has the effect of thinning and weakening the layer in that area, so that when it is blown it stretches more easily (c). A final gather of clear glass can be made over the top (d).

Fig. 49. *Attaching a disc of coloured glass to the gather produces a half coloured effect.*

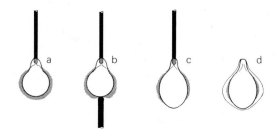

Fig. 50. *Varying the intensity of colours.*

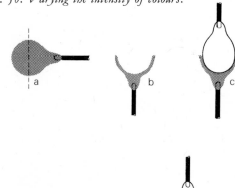

Fig. 48. *Casing from the tank.*

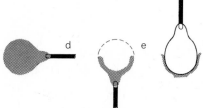

Fig. 51. *Flashing with two irons.*

57

Opposite above: dish with blue glass fragments included from the marver. Ray Flavell.

Opposite below: two bowls with red glass included from the marver. Ray Flavell.

This page: stages in making a decorative tile.

Top left: a gather is dropped into a metal frame placed on the marver.

Middle: a pattern is impressed with a metal object.

Right: the glass cooling from red heat in the frame.

Below: the piece removed from the frame ready for annealing.

CASING AND FLASHING WITH TWO IRONS

(Fig. 51.) A sufficiently large bulb of crystal glass, cased in colour as previously described, is blown to a thin wide shape, transferred to a punty and cracked off at its widest part (a). The open end is then further widened (b) and a second bulb of clear metal blown inside its hollow form (c). It is essential in this process that the two layers join without trapping air.

Alternatively, the coloured form need not be removed to a punty. It may be blown to a thin section on the pipe and then held vertically so that it collapses inside itself (e). The second clear glass form is then blown inside the hollow shape (f) and the unwanted outer shape cracked off.

There is little problem involved in casing if the glassmaker has two furnaces, but where only one exists improvised methods will have to be employed. Small quantities of coloured glass can be melted in the working hole in a metal pan – preferably made of stainless steel which does not scale. As soon as the glass is soft enough it can be gathered on the end of an iron and worked in the ways described.

VARIEGATED GLASS

A simple method is to throw into the pot coloured glass rods which, as soon as they have softened, can be gathered in the usual way. The resultant vessels will be multi-coloured but some coloured material may remain to contaminate future batches.

MAKING THE GLASS IRIDESCENT

Iridescence is produced by allowing the surface of the metal, while still hot from the furnace, to be attacked by the fumes of stannous chloride. The surface layer of glass undergoes certain chemical changes which allow it to absorb some of the rays of the spectrum. Thus the colours observed are complementary to those which have been absorbed. The iridescence is caused by variation in thickness of the attacked glass layer, and the effect shows up best in dark coloured glasses. The degree of attack is dependent on time and temperature.

The process is easy to carry out. The stannous chloride can be heated on a metal tray, a common practice being to drop a blob of molten metal into it. Best results are obtained in a fuming chamber made up as in Fig. 77. This comprises a muffle which admits the form on the punty and closes round it. A flue leads into the chamber, and an extraction flue leads out of it. The receptacle for the stannous chloride (an iron ladle is adequate) can be pre-heated in the furnace mouth. Just before the piece is cracked off from the punty it is reheated to cherry red and inserted into the chamber. The stannous chloride powder is then dropped into the heated ladle at the base of the lower flue so that the fumes flow upwards into the muffle and then pass out of the upper flue.

ENAMELS

A wide range of bright colours is available from enamels manufacturers. They are composed of colouring agents, usually metallic oxides, and fluxes combined with silica. Glass enamels are applied to the surface of glass and fuse on during a second firing to about 600° C.

For brush painting they may be purchased ready ground and mixed with medium. Alternatively they may be purchased in powder form, ground in turpentine on a ceramic tile with a palette knife until all grittiness disappears, and then mixed with various oils to give degrees of 'fattiness' to the brush stroke. To produce even brush strokes, enamels need to be as fine as possible and those which are sold for lithographic transfer making are recommended because they are very finely ground.

Bright gold and silver lustres may be painted on and fired at the same temperatures. Various proprietary resists may be employed. Special enamels can be used to build up an image in relief. Manufacturers issue instructions with their materials and these should be followed.

Glass enamels may contain a high lead content which is poisonous. Manufacturers' advice should be sought when using them.

Cold Methods of Decoration

GLASS CUTTING

The glass cutter's wheel is attached to a spindle which rotates relatively slowly. While there may be provision for changing drive ratios for various sizes of wheels, the speed is not generally varied during the cutting operation. To a great extent, the shape and contour of the cutting edge determine the character of the cut. Generally, wheels are made with three types of edge:
1. convex, which makes a hollow rounded cut
2. bevel, which is used for V cuts
3. flat, which is used for flat cuts

Most commonly a V sectioned cut is made, the facets of which refract the light to produce a sparkling effect. Traditionally the technique is used for straight, non-continuous cuts, and therefore designs, because they are assemblages of these, tend to be geometric. Variation and interest are given to the cutting by the way the contours of the vessel intersect those of the cutting wheel.

CAUTION:
It is essential that large wheels are secured by flanges to prevent break-up, and eye protection should be worn in all cutting operations.

The design is first marked on with a chinagraph type pencil and is then 'roughed in' by holding it against the *top* surface of the wheel. The wheel may be of metal or, more usually, carborundum. On metal wheels, the cutting effect is produced by trailing a mixture of sharp sand and water to the edge of the disc, just in front of the area of contact. The cut so produced is very rough and requires further treatment on a second wheel. This is known as fine

Fig. 52. Glass cutting. Initial deep cutting. Photo: Glass Manufacturers' Federation.

cutting and is carried out on a wheel of sandstone or bonded material. Its effect is to remove the roughness of the first cut and to leave a smooth but opaque surface. It is possible to leave all or part of the cutting in this state, but if a polished surface is required the work has to be subjected to a final polishing process. If the design is fairly open, first polishing may be done on a wooden disc fed with pumice and water. This puts a first polish on the larger areas. More usually, the ware is held against revolving felt or cork discs fed with pumice, the final brilliance being obtained by 'putty polishing'. The putty is a mixture of lead and tin oxides applied to the wheel.

Fig. 53. *Cut glass decanter. English crystal, about 1845.*
Photo: Victoria and Albert Museum. (Opposite).

Fig. 54. *Cut crystal vases by Olle Alberius. Orrefors*
Glasbruk.

Fig. 55. Intaglio cutting. Photo: Glass Manufacturers' Federation. (Above).

Fig. 56. Copper wheel engraving. Photo: Glass Manufacturers' Federation. (Below).

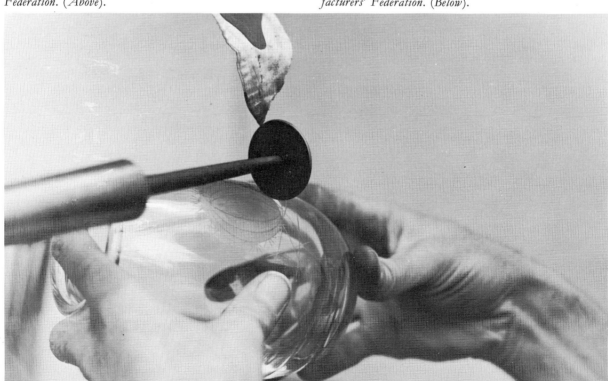

Fig. 57. Engraved crystal bowl by Ray Flavell.

INTAGLIO CUTTING

Intaglio cutting is a similar process employing smaller wheels. It does not make such deep cuts and so makes for a much lighter form of decoration.

A variable speed lathe provides the power, but instead of metal wheels, carborundum stones are attached to the spindle. The work is held underneath the disc, and water only is fed to the cutting surface.

Felt wheels for polishing may be fitted to the same shaft.

ENGRAVING

Glass engraving is a very old process. Various copper wheels, ranging in size from $\frac{1}{4}$ in. to 3 in. diameter, can be attached to a spindle which has a variable speed drive or a kick type crank operated by the engraver.

The copper wheel is fed with emery powder in oil,

65

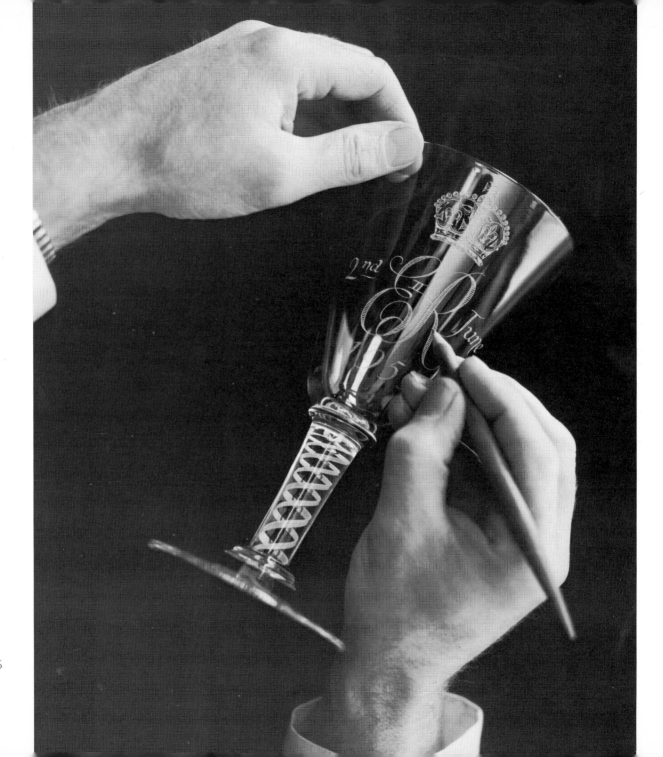

and the article being engraved is held against the *underside* of the wheel. The engraved surface is smooth but mat and is generally left unpolished. Engraving is more flexible than glass cutting: because it makes only a shallow cut, the wheel can be used in a more graphic manner. Designs can incorporate continuous curved lines. By changing the copper wheels, different effects can be achieved. A dentist's drill can be adapted for glass engraving. The process is commonly used on full lead crystal.

DIAMOND ENGRAVING

A diamond, or more usually a tungsten carbide tip, mounted on a stylus, can be used to cut the surface of glass. The mark is more in the nature of a scratch and a pictorial treatment is achieved by building up an image with stippled effects. As the pattern relies on its opacifying effect, it is never polished.

ETCHING

Glass is highly resistant to most acids except hydro-fluoric, which attacks it vigorously; the silicates are broken down and the gas silicon fluoride is given off. The degree of attack varies with the type of glass, full lead crystal glasses being more easily dissolved than the harder potash glasses. In most cases, silica fluoride salts from the lead, lime or potash are deposited on the surface and have to be cleared constantly or the glass will take on a mat look. Sometimes other acids are added to assist the hydrofluoric, for example nitric for lead glasses and sulphuric for

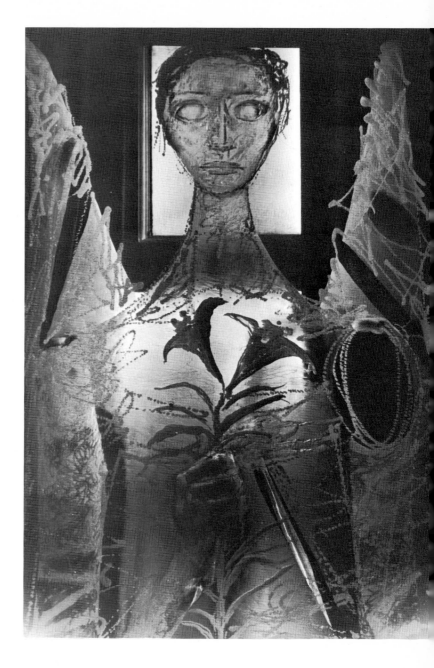

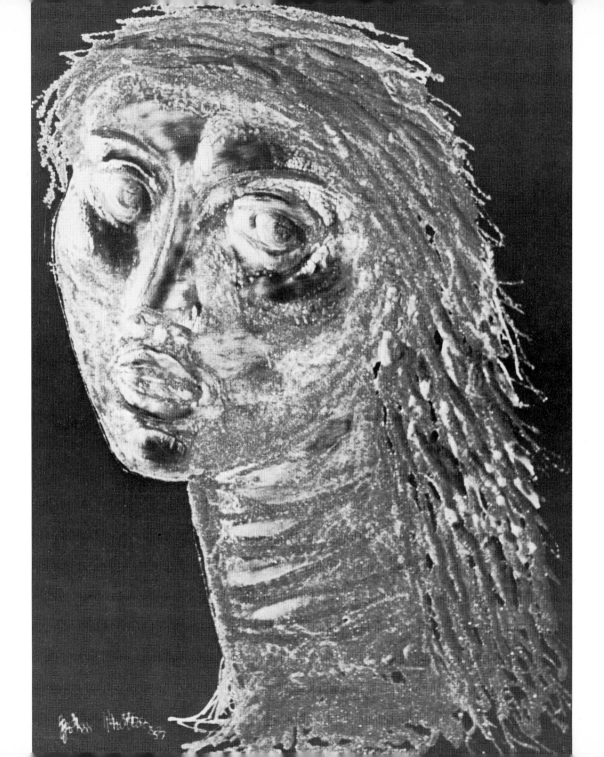

68

lime glasses. Typical etching recipes are given in Table 3.

CAUTION:

As these mixtures attack silicates, glass or pottery containers are dissolved but lead containers are not. The mixtures are caustic, and normal precautions for handling acids should be taken. As they give off noxious vapours, they should be stored in a fume cupboard. If in doubt, specialist advice should be sought. Also seek advice about waste disposal.

Etched patterns are produced by masking off those areas which are not required to be attacked by the acid. For this purpose, various resists can be applied: wax is satisfactory, the design being easily scribed through to expose the underlying glass surface. Proprietary wax compounds can be purchased, but a mixture of beeswax and turpentine is satisfactory.

STAMPING

An etching solution can be applied to a suitable flexible form and stamped on to the surface of the ware. For this purpose, a concentrated solution of ammonium fluoride in hydrofluoric acid is recommended. Patterns can be carved into rubber or cast from latex or PVC compounds.

Table 2
COMPARISON OF WHEELS USED IN GLASS DECORATION
(from data supplied by Glassworks Equipment Ltd.)

TYPE	WHEEL DIAMETER		SPEED RANGE RPM		TYPE	MAX. WT. LBS.	REMARKS
	MIN.	MAX.	MIN.	MAX.			
Rough cutting	3	16	725	1750	Carborundum	25	Used for long straight cuts to be followed by smooth cutting. Speed change usually by stepped pulleys or infinitely variable speed pulley system.
Smooth/fine cutting	3	16	185	1080	Carborundum	25	Used to finish rough cutting. Speed change usually by stepped pulleys or infinitely variable speed pulley system.
Intaglio	1	10	232	2500	Carborundum	3	Used for light cuts, straight or curved. Infinitely variable speed, mechanical drive.
Puntying (rough)	4	8	232	1550	Carborundum	5	Used for grinding punty marks from bases. Usually about 1 in. wide. Mechanical drive. Stepless speed change.
Puntying (smooth)	4	8	232	1550	Carborundum	5	Used for smoothing rough punty cuts. Mechanical drive, stepless speed change.
Engraving	Standard engraving shank 6H7		2800	12000	Diamond or carborundum		Used for graphic surface decoration.

N.B. *The above information refers to 30% lead crystal and is not necessarily correct for lower lead content glasses as manufactured in Europe and the U.S.A.*

Table 3
ETCHING RECIPES

	SODA GLASS	LEAD GLASS	MAT ETCH	STAMPING PASTE	POLISHING
CONC. HYDROFLUORIC ACID	1	0	0	5	3·5
CONC. NITRIC ACID	0	1	0	0	0
CONC. SULPHURIC ACID	1	1	0	0	6·5
WATER	8	8	8·9	0	0
HYDROCHLORIC ACID	0	0	0·1	0	0
POTASSIUM FLUORIDE	0	0	1	0	0
AMMONIUM FLUORIDE	0	0	0	5	0

ACID POLISHING

Mat glass can be made glossy by immersion in acid, and a typical recipe is shown in Table 3. The article should be alternately immersed in the acid and warm water until the desired polish has been obtained. The precipitation of the salt crystals on the surface gives a mat effect and can be encouraged if a fluoride is added to the etching solution. The solution may be applied by brush or by dipping – in either case, it takes rather a long time. For best results, a constant temperature of 60° C is advised.

SAND BLASTING

An effect not dissimilar to the mat etching of fluorides is obtained by sand blasting techniques. Sand blasting machines are of various types but they all operate on the principle that sharp sand is driven at high velocity to impinge on the surface of the glass. This has the effect of abrading the surface very rapidly. To produce a pattern by this process, it is necessary to

70

Fig. 60. Sandblasted bowl in colour by Bertil Vallien, AB Åforsgruppen. The shape is cased in coloured glass and the decoration sandblasted back to the clear glass.

Fig. 61. Sandblasted and acid polished vase in full crystal by Ray Flavell. (Opposite).

mask off part of the glass surface so that the resultant pattern quality is one of contrast between the mat exposed surface and the glossy surface which has been protected.

Masks can be made of thin sheet zinc which is easily formed around contours and cut with a stencil knife. Masking tape can be used for individual pieces. Proprietary latex based materials can be painted on the surface: when their solvents evaporate a rubbery skin remains which can be cut with a stencil knife. Small articles are usually worked in a cabinet which has provision for handling the ware but which protects the operator. Larger objects may be worked in the open, but the operator must wear protective clothing. Various grades of grit, sand etc. may be used to give different effects.

Fig. 62. Glass vessel, probably Spanish, 18th to 19th century, showing a variety of techniques for applied decoration. Photo: Victoria and Albert Museum.

Chapter 6

Glassworking without a Furnace

If it is desired to manipulate hollow glass forms of reasonable size in the molten state then a furnace is essential, but much interesting work can be done using stock forms of glass (sheet, rod, tube etc.) in a potter's kiln or by direct local heating in the flame of a blowtorch. Even scrap glass can be put to use.

Kiln Fired Methods

Glass can be softened in a potter's kiln but the worker is unable to see the forming in progress. Control can only be exercised by varying the heating and cooling cycle, though with experience it is possible to anticipate fairly accurately the effect a particular firing programme will have on different thicknesses and types of glass. Most forms of flat glass can be reworked in a variety of ways but the simplest technique, and one which offers considerable scope, is lamination. If two sheets of glass are fired on top of each other they fuse together, and if suitable decorative material or colour is placed between the two layers it will, after firing, be embedded in the middle of the solid.

SEPARATORS

One fundamental problem arises with kiln fired methods: the glass must somehow be supported in the fused state. Adhesions are obviated by the use of a separator. This can be any inert powder which has a higher melting point than glass. Commonly, cristobalite (a form of silica), alumina or whiting (calcium carbonate) are used. Such materials can be purchased as proprietary compounds for coating shelves of pottery kilns to prevent glaze adhesions. Separators are best made up with water containing a small amount of gum to act as a binder. They can be applied by spraying, dipping or brushing. Alternatively, flat surfaces can be coated by dusting through a muslin bag.

Flat glass laminates are best fired on sillimanite kiln shelves: these tend to remain flatter than the fireclay types.

FIRING TECHNIQUE

When firing a potter's kiln it is advisable to remove the bungs for the initial period of the firing so that harmful gases can escape. The degree of distortion or fusion of glass is governed by:
1. the time the piece is subjected to heat
2. the highest temperature achieved
3. the make-up of the particular glass

It should be noted that temperature alone does not determine the degree of movement; time is also important. As metallic oxides are strong fluxes, many coloured glasses have a lower melting point than clear glasses. No hard and fast guide to temperatures can be given but typical effects at various points of the schedule are given in Table 4, p. 90.

DRAPE-FORMING LAMINATES INTO RELIEF

Flat sheet glass placed over a suitable hump-mould softens during firing and becomes draped around the mould. Any rigid material which withstands the temperatures involved can be used for the mould, though the commonest and most versatile is potter's clay. Most kinds of clay can be used but the most suitable is an open textured stoneware type containing a high proportion of grog. A suitable material can be purchased ready prepared, and a fireclay or a mixture of sand and plaster can also be used. Sheet glass will drape over quite steep contours providing the form is not too complex. Moulds may be modelled by hand, and circular shapes can be made on a potter's wheel. They should be prefired and coated with a separator. Before placing, glass blanks should be cut to fit the mould outline.

73

LAMINATING COLOURS

Enamel colours for ceramics fire at about 750° C and glass enamels fire at about 560–580° C. Above these temperatures many colours (notably pinks, reds, the lighter colours and liquid gold and silver lustres) fire out. Most other colours (blues, greens, browns and darker shades) will withstand higher temperatures and can be used successfully in laminates. Colours which have been formulated as underglaze colours for ceramics, and which are designed to withstand glost temperatures, are easiest to use and offer the best range for glass laminating.

Patterns which are complex or symmetrical are best drawn on paper and the glass blank superimposed so that the design can be copied through. Colours can be painted but brush painting does not always deposit sufficient pigment, and it is more satisfactory to paint the image in a heavy bodied oil and to dust powdered pigment on to the tacky surface this provides. Crushed glass can be applied in this way.

FLUXES

Because colours which are laminated are sandwiched between two glass layers, it is not normally necessary to adjust their fusion temperatures with fluxes. Even plain metallic oxides can be used. But where vitrified coatings are required on outer glass surfaces, fluxes may be required to assist fusion. Fluxes can also be added to ground up glass to assist complete fusion. Various proprietary brands are available but the following recipe may prove useful for most purposes.

Lead oxide 50%
Silica 37%
Boric oxide 10%
Soda 3%

TRAPPING BUBBLES IN LAMINATES

It is relatively easy to produce a regular pattern of bubbles in a laminate. Powdered clear glass mixed with a little flux is applied to oiled stripes across each blank. These stripes are put together at right angles to

Fig. 63a and b. Metal gauze laminated.

each other to produce a 'criss-cross' effect, the uncovered spaces forming the bubbles during the firing. Mica flakes can also be laid on the interface to produce bubbles. These puff up during the firing and eventually disappear leaving bubbles.

FURTHER MATERIALS FOR LAMINATING

Thin wire structures, even wire mesh, can be cut to shape and successfully laminated, though some wires oxidise and look black. The wires can be extended beyond the edge of the glass and used for suspension. Aluminium foil laminates easily although it tends to oxidise. Sand, particularly in the finer grades, often produces an iridescent effect. Strands of glass fibre dipped in underglaze colour produce an effect like embedded threads.

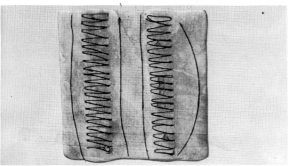

Fig. 64a and b. Nickel chrome wire laminated.

TRAILED GLAZES

Coloured pottery glazes which fire at low temperature should be mixed to a creamy consistency and sieved before being trailed from a potter's slip-trailer. A baby's feeding bottle fitted with a nozzle at one end and mouth-blown at the other makes an easily controlled tool. A variety of proprietary glazes with an excellent range of colours is readily available from manufacturers.

FUSING BOTTLE-GLASS

Common bottles can easily be caused to collapse into a flat form by heating them to softening point. If placed over a mould, they will even take up the form

of the mould. Coloured glass fragments, glass beads etc. placed inside before firing lend added interest.

Lampworking

This is the manipulation of glass in an open flame. It may be familiar already to those who are acquainted with the chemistry laboratory: the technique is employed by skilled craftsmen to make complex assemblies for scientific purposes – condensers, vacuum pumps, burettes etc. Nowadays the technique seems to be used largely for the making of glass animals and trinkets for the giftware trade, and for glass eyes.

Glass rod in a variety of colours and sections may be purchased from manufacturers. To start with, cane of about $\frac{1}{4}$ in. and $\frac{1}{2}$ in. diameter and tube of about $\frac{1}{2}$ in. diameter should be purchased. The techniques employed by lampworkers are highly personal. For this reason the novice will learn best from his own experience and he is encouraged to discover for himself the behaviour and feel of glass as it is heated in an open flame. Any glass will flow if heated past its

Fig. 65. Lampwork. Fusing glass tubing to complete a distillation tube. Photo: Glass Manufacturers' Federation.

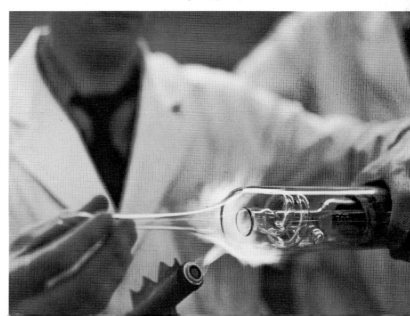

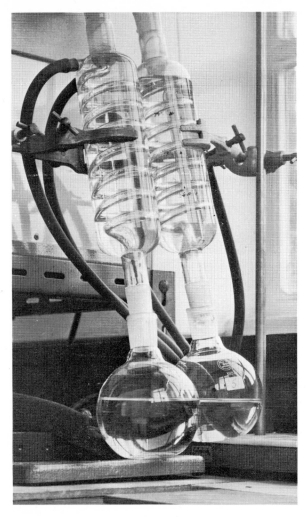

Fig. 66. Chemical apparatus made by lampworking.

softening point, and the art of lampworking, as indeed with other forms of glassmaking, is to control the material when it is in the molten state.

Before commencing work, ensure that the burner is securely fixed and adjusted to a blue flame. (Follow manufacturers' instructions for lighting and adjust-

ing.) The newcomer will soon learn how sharp edges can be softened, that tube can easily be sealed, and that cane and tube can readily be drawn into thin sections. A thickness in the mid-section of cane can be built up by softening that area and pressing the ends together. Alternatively, a local thickness can be built up by winding on a thread from another cane and fusing the thickened mass in a hot flame. If about 2 in. of the end of a sealed glass tube is heated, a small bulb can be blown, though this will necessarily be small because there is insufficient material in the walls of the tube to provide for the larger form. If the end of the tube is first thickened by trailing on a thread, a larger bulb can be formed.

Coloured threaded rod can be made as follows. Heat 2 in. of the end of a piece of clear cane, and on to this softened area fuse a few strips of thin drawn coloured cane. Reheat and marver until the coloured material is completely fused into the clear base. Nip the end to a point and to the point attach a $\frac{1}{4}$ in. cane. Slowly draw the two pieces apart maintaining a twisting action at the same time. Coloured spots may be applied to a form simply by 'touching on' $\frac{1}{4}$ in. cane and drawing it away as soon as it has fused. The spots so deposited will need to be softened by reheating. The making of composite pieces has to be planned so that all operations can be carried out whilst the work is attached to a glass stem, even though it frequently passes from one stem to another as the various parts are attached.

EQUIPMENT REQUIRED

The equipment needed for lampworking is minimal, the burner being the only major item required. This may be fired by town gas and air, or by butane or propane from cylinders such as are supplied for caravans. Advice on the most suitable burner should

Fig. 67. 'Icicles' by Barry Cullen, student at Hammersmith College of Building. Glass rods of different diameters are fired to about 800° F and mounted in a frame. Photo: Barry Cullen. (Opposite).

77

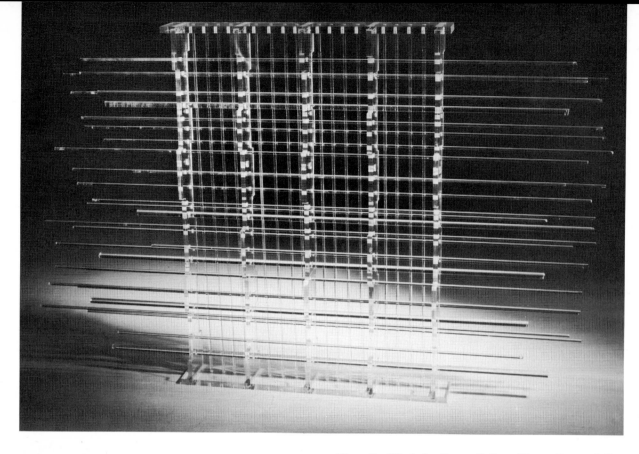

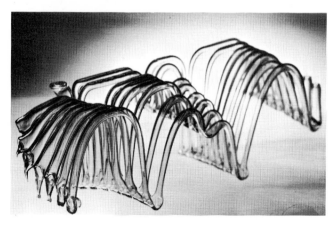

Fig. 68. Work by Barry Cullen. Photo: Barry Cullen. (Above).

be sought from the local Gas Board where a supply already exists, or from a proprietary cylinder gas supplier. The burner must be capable of mounting so that the flame is vertical.

CAUTION:
Where gas cylinders are employed, they should be stored outside where they cannot be tampered with.

Figs. 69, 70 and 71. Work by students of Foley College of Art, Stourbridge. (Left and opposite).

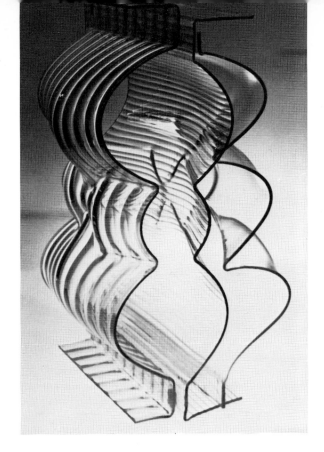

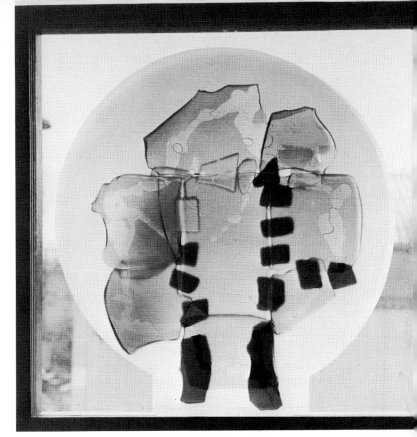

Additional small hand tools advised are:
Small glassmaker's forceps
Goggles as recommended by gas supplier
Sharp nosed pliers
Small glassmaker's shears
Fine triangular file for cutting off
Cone for flaring ends
Asbestos gloves
Asbestos topped work table
Scrap-bin made of metal
Shaping tools as required

Chapter 7

Setting up a Workshop

No great expenditure is involved in setting up a glass workshop. The furnace is the most expensive item and one can be constructed with ease by any fairly practical person. Because of the fire hazard, the workshop, and particularly the floor, should be constructed of materials of low flammability. It must be well ventilated.

The Glassmaker's Chair

(Fig. 72.) The glassmaker usually adapts this to suit himself, but it can be constructed from angle iron or wood to the dimensions shown. The seat is extended

Fig. 72. The glassmaker's chair.

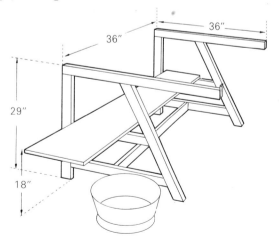

to provide a platform for hand tools. Wooden tools are stored in water in a tank placed behind this. Note the metal tray or bin placed below the working area to receive trimmings – this is essential for safety. It is usual to erect a metal shield along the working side of the bench to protect the operator. If the chair is constructed of angle iron, it is advised that a wooden insert is placed in the 'arms' opposite the work side: the additional friction makes for a better rolling action and prevents the pipe from 'skidding'. If the arms are made of wood, it is good practice to attach a metal edge to the workside 'arm' to prevent the wood from burning.

The Glassmaker's Hand Tools

BLOWING - IRONS
(Fig. 73.) These are made of mild steel tube of about $\frac{5}{8}$ in. diameter, thicker at the gathering end and tapered at the blowing end. They come in various lengths and thicknesses but the novice working out of a small tank is advised to obtain irons about 5 ft. long. Better quality irons are made in stainless steel which, because of its lower thermal conductivity, remains cooler in working. Irons must be quite straight otherwise the nose will not stay centred when working on the arms of the chair.

PUNTIES
Punties are usually smaller in diameter than irons – about $\frac{3}{8}$ in. Blown glass pieces are transferred to these from the blowing-irons so that necks and rims can be finished. They are also used for making small gathers which are not to be blown. They are available with specially treated tips but the novice will be able to make his own from mild steel rod.

SHEARS
(Fig. 75.) Two types are essential: one for trimming the edges of glass shapes and the other for cutting off lengths of glass. Trimming shears are not unlike metal shears but because metal shears have no loops

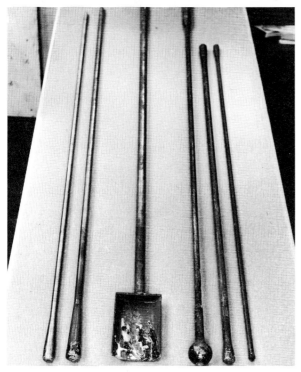

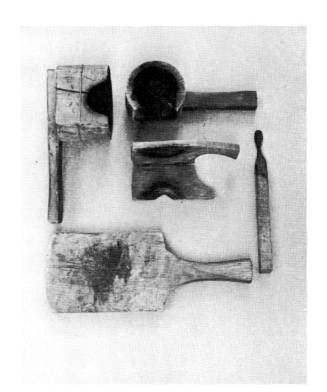

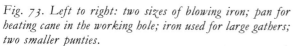

Fig. 73. Left to right: two sizes of blowing iron; pan for heating cane in the working hole; iron used for large gathers; two smaller punties.

on the handles they are difficult to use quickly. 'Parrot nosed' or 'cut-off' shears are recessed so that they grip the glass during the cutting operation. They often have nips at the very end which are used for steadying punty irons when positioning handles etc.

TONGS

(Fig. 75.) These are sometimes known as 'jacks' or

Fig. 74. Three cup moulds and a paddle. (Right above).
Fig. 75. Shears and tongs. Top: two pairs of tongs. Left to right: 'cut-off' shears with end nips; two sizes of trimming shears; and tongs with wooden bits. (Right below).

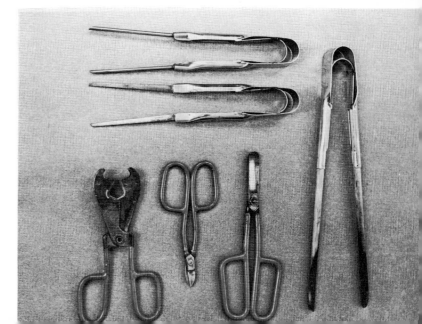

'pucellas'. They are mostly used for opening necks or for grooving forms. Those fitted with wooden end-bits tend to mark the glass least, but from time to time the wooden bits have to be replaced. Sometimes they are made of green willow wood.

FILES

These may be used to score the glass when it is time to crack off the piece. Coarse files are unsuitable; sharp fine files are best, preferably about 1 ft. long.

PADDLES

(Fig. 74.) These are flat pieces of wood with handles, used for flattening glass forms. They must be considered expendable. The glassmaker usually makes up his own shapes.

BLOCKING MOULDS

(Fig. 74.) Generally made of beech or fruit wood, these may be turned on a lathe or hand carved. They are used for making the gather symmetrical.

HOOKS

These are mostly used for purposes of decoration, such as drawing different coloured threads into a feathered effect or for 'spiking' to make air bubbles.

MARVER

(Fig. 76.) This is the flat metal bed on which molten glass is rolled. It should be fixed at a height convenient to the operator and must be firm and steady. Heated marvers which chill the glass less are available for special purpose work.

ANNEALING OVEN

See annealing, p. 38.

FUMING MUFFLE

This is used for making the glass iridescent by subjecting it to the fumes of stannous chloride (see p. 60). It can be constructed as in Fig. 77.

Fig. 76. The marver.

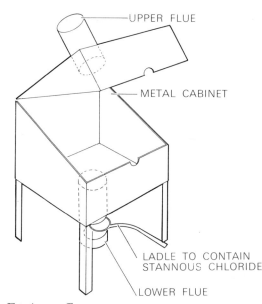

UPPER FLUE

METAL CABINET

LADLE TO CONTAIN STANNOUS CHLORIDE

LOWER FLUE

Fig. 77. Fuming muffle.

GLORY-HOLE

This book has dealt with glassworking with limited facilities, but the stage is soon reached when a glory-hole becomes essential. The glory-hole is a chamber in which work on the iron can be reheated. So far it has been said that work can be reheated in the furnace-mouth, but with this method it is not possible to limit the area being heated. For better control it is essential to be able to heat local areas, and this can be done in the glory-hole.

It consists simply of a metal cylinder lined with refractory materials and fitted with gas burners which provide an even heat. It should run at about 1400° C – considerably higher than the working temperature of the glass furnace. The internal diameter may be about 14 in. but it is common practice to place over the opening refractory slabs with restricted apertures which match the shapes being blown.

The equipment can readily be improvised using an old oil drum lined with refractories. The local Gas Board will advise on burners if they are told the volume and shape of the inside, the area of the opening, the wall material and its thickness, and the method of ventilating.

CAUTION:
The glare from the glory-hole is harmful to the eyes, and work should only be observed through protective glasses.

GRINDER

Flat grinding can be done by hand on any hard flat surface with carborundum paste, though the process is tedious. It is far better to make up some form of powered revolving surface. A potter's wheel fitted with a large turntable and set to run at low speed can be improvised as in Fig. 78. Alternatively, the turntable can be driven by an electric motor with a suitable reduction drive.

CAUTION:
When flat grinding, a stage may be reached where air is excluded from between the surfaces and it becomes difficult to part the piece from the grinder. In this condition, the piece can easily be snatched out of the operator's hands. The grinding surface must therefore be well wetted with water.

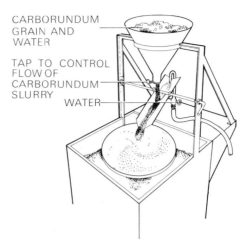

CARBORUNDUM
GRAIN AND
WATER

TAP TO CONTROL
FLOW OF
CARBORUNDUM
SLURRY

WATER

Fig. 78. Potter's wheel adapted as horizontal mill or grinder.

GLASS CUTTING AND ENGRAVING EQUIPMENT
Specialised equipment is available commercially and manufacturers' advice should be sought.

MOULDS
These can easily be improvised; Figs. 79–82 illustrate typical examples. A potter's jigger and jolley can be adapted to make a lever press for press-moulding as in Fig. 83. (Note that the mould does not rotate.)

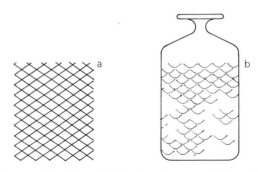

Fig. 79a. Simple mould fabricated of expanded metal; b. typical glass moulding.

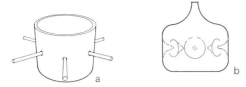

Fig. 80a. Mould; b. moulding. (Holes in the cylinder locate metal rods which make depressions in the moulding.)

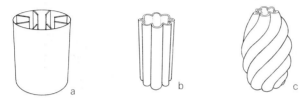

Fig. 81a. Simple fabricated mould; b and c. typical mouldings.

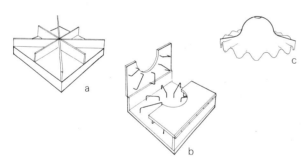

Fig. 82a and b. Crimping moulds; c. typical moulding.

CAST
ALUMINIUM MOULD
(FIXED)

DIE

Fig. 83. Potter's jigger and jolley adapted as a lever press.

Construction of a Furnace

Details are given below for the construction of a small tank type furnace suitable for studio and workshop use. It is fired by gas and forced air. No flue is required but, to carry away the products of combustion, a hood fitted with an extractor unit is necessary. The mouth of the furnace should never be completely closed or the products of combustion will be unable to escape.

The furnace mainly consists of a tank of about 1 cu. ft. capacity made in highly refractory bricks, surmounted by a chamber also made of refractory material, which not only provides access for the blowing-irons but also forms a heated box or glory-hole in which work can be reheated on the pipe. The whole is encased in a layer of insulation bricks. The burner is mounted inverted in the roof of the chamber.

Dimensions are not critical; the working-hole should be about waist high for the operator and can

Fig. 84. General layout of brickwork for a furnace.

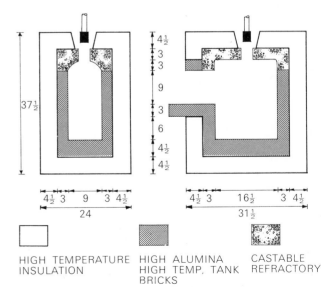

HIGH TEMPERATURE INSULATION

HIGH ALUMINA HIGH TEMP. TANK BRICKS

CASTABLE REFRACTORY

be adjusted by varying the height of the metal stand which supports the brickwork. The size of the upper chamber used for reheating will be quite adequate for normal purposes, but if it is required to make larger pieces its size will have to be increased.

CONSTRUCTION

(See Figs. 84–98.) All bricks used in the furnace are 9 in. × $4\frac{1}{2}$ in. × 3 in. and dimensions can be calculated from the photographs; the high temperature bricks look darker here than the insulation bricks. Vacuum cast bricks are preferred: because of their low permeability, these offer greater resistance to glass attack.

87

85

88

86

85

D

89

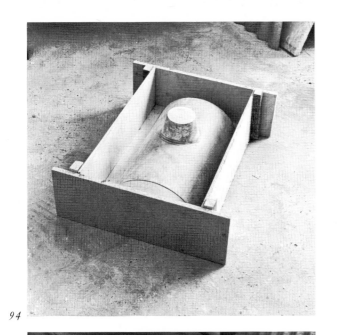

98

No mortar is used; bricks are laid dry but the best possible close packing and fit should be aimed at to prevent gaps. The structure must also be quite square and vertical to receive the angle-irons and tie-bars. Where possible, joints should be staggered. This prevents structural weakness and gaps which permit heat losses. Insulation bricks are easily cut with multi-purpose saws and rasps.

Fig. 85
A substantial metal frame is constructed out of either welded angle-iron or bolted slotted-angle, and located so that the mouth of the furnace will face the required direction. (It is desirable to arrange for plenty of clear space in front of the furnace.)
Fig. 86.
On this is laid a sheet of asbestos material about 1 in. thick, and on this in turn is laid the first layer of insulation bricks. Note that those in the middle are laid on their narrow edges, thus preventing the joints from coinciding with those of the outer layer.

Figs. 87 and 88
The tank is then constructed from refractory brick, with inside measurements of approximately 9 in. high × 15 in. deep × 9 in. wide. Fig. 87 shows the base of the tank laid and Fig. 88 shows the sides of the tank completed. Insulating bricks are placed around the tank, particular care being taken in this area that joints do not coincide and that the outer corners are square and vertical. In the pictures, the high temperature bricks can be seen to protrude into the insulation. This merely assists bonding.
Fig. 89
The upper chamber is now built up to accommodate the furnace mouth, which in this case has been made 9 in. × 9 in. for ease of construction.
Figs. 90 and 91
The insulation brick is cut to size with a saw to fill gaps.
Fig. 92
Note that two high temperature refractory bricks are placed in front of the working hole to provide a hearth.
Fig. 93
The lintel is placed over the working hole, and insulation is shown part laid around the tank.
Fig. 94
A mould for the arch of the chamber is made out of plywood and blockboard. The circular piece on the top will form the hole for the burner, and should be enlarged to allow ½ in. clearance all round. The burner must be located over the centre of the tank.
Fig. 95
The chamber arch is made of castable refractory material. Manufacturers' instructions for mixing should be followed. A slab can be cast separately to provide a block for the working hole, which must have a vent.
Fig. 96
The arch is carefully positioned over the chamber.
Fig. 97
The encasing in insulation brick is completed. Note that at least ½ in. clearance around the burner should

Fig. 105. *Blown bottles by Bertil Vallien.*

what is applied to one side of a transparent vessel is seen in reverse through the other, the image being distorted and reflected many times in a kaleidoscopic effect. Considerations of the surface treatment of glass clearly cannot be separated from those of the underlying form – they are one and the same.

Form in glass is much related to thickness, not only in the way each contributes to the distortion and reflection of light, but because one is dependent on the other in the making process: thick sections do not inflate as easily as thin ones and, when making

Fig. 106. *'Eye', glass sculpture by Ann and Göran Wärf.*

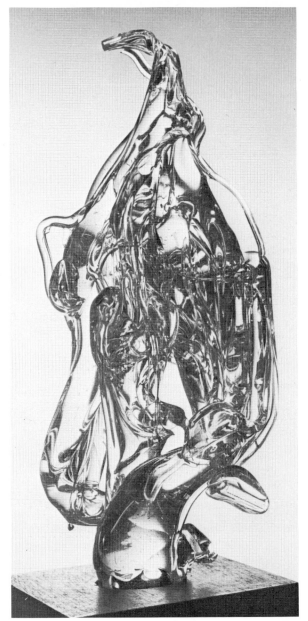

Figs. *107* and *108. Examples of work produced by students after a few days of practice. Photo: West Surrey College of Art and Design. (Opposite).*
Fig. *109. Candle holder in crystal by Olle Alberius for Orrefors Glasbruk. Mould blown. (Below).*

Fig. *110. Crystal decanters by Olle Alberius for Orrefors Glasbruk.*

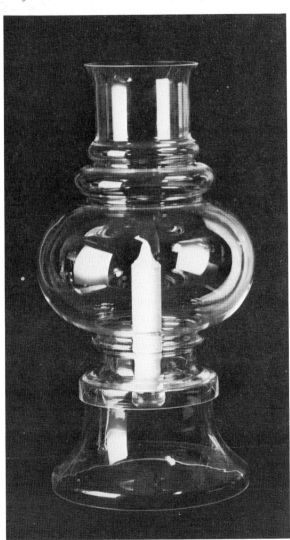

Fig. 111. Solid crystal glass block. Sven Palmquist for Orrefors Glasbruk.

Fig. 112. Crystal goblet by Ray Flavell.

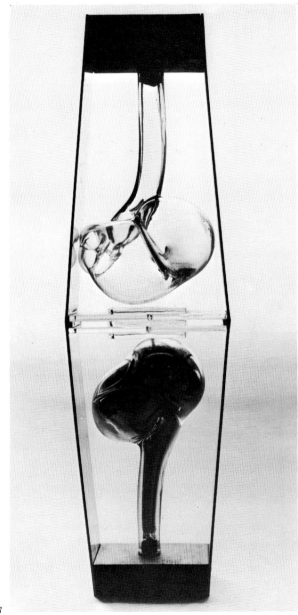

114

Figs. 113–118. Pieces by Sam Herman.

'off hand' pieces, any irregularities of thickness in the parison develop as irregularities of form. Good 'off hand' pieces, as opposed to moulded pieces, seem to retain the quality of fluidity of the molten state; the form is not static. In the molten state, glass is always on the move, live and demanding. Its final form is determined when the glassmaker decides to arrest all movement by allowing it to cool. Good glassblowing is immediate, involving the minimum necessary number of steps from the gather to the final form. If a shape has only been achieved after much manipulation and adjustment, it looks limp and contrived. For

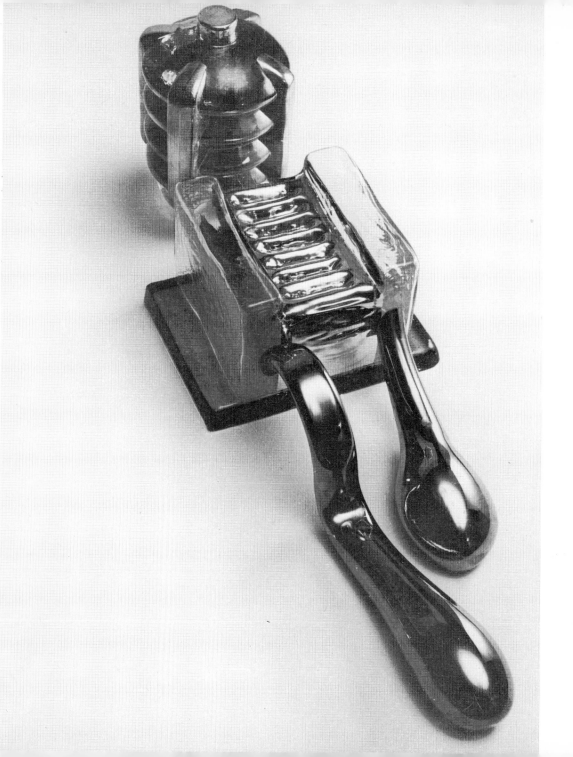

117

this reason, glass forms are best designed in the molten state; it is inappropriate to start with static silhouettes on the drawing board for later translation into three dimensions. Few worthwhile pieces have been made 'one off' at the first attempt; mostly the better forms are selected from several which have been made towards a basic concept.

The glassworker discovers that whenever simple, direct movements are applied, glass tends to take up a satisfying form naturally; a plain gob drawn out inevitably results in a pleasantly waisted shape. If this is allowed to fall over of its own accord it will take up a curve or a twist which is appropriate (at the right moment) for its section and mass. If a form is swung on an iron it will elongate naturally. Thus the relatively unskilled worker may be able to produce pleasant enough sculptural forms by working the material in simple direct movements, assisting it to follow its natural inclinations or maintaining the equilibrium as necessary. Indeed this could be

described as the essence of glassblowing, but it is a far cry from the skills possessed by the experts and the 'gaffers' whose distinctive ability is to make a piece to a *predetermined* size and form and to *repeat* it.

Truly symmetrical shapes are difficult to make and can look very tired if they are attempted 'one off' by the artist glassmaker. It must be remembered that most hand made symmetrical shapes (mainly tableware) are made by teams of men who repeat the same limited range day in, day out. Within their sphere they are experts; they can gather exactly the right amount of metal and work from the parison to the finished form swiftly and directly with the minimum number of operations and with the utmost economy of movement. The resultant forms, if impersonal and unimaginative, are positive and spontaneous.

Up to now, the majority of glass forms have been produced by teams of such craftsmen; the individual craftsman or studio glassmaker is a recent phenomenon who is not (or should not be) attempting to imitate his industrial counterpart either in expertise or final product. Already we see the exploratory work of the individual glass artists: shapes are cut to reveal their inner surfaces; forms are dissected and reassembled; sculptures are made of solid ground glass; there is an infinite variety of treatments in the hot state and sometimes glass is used in innovatory ways with other materials. A great deal of it is well done and very exciting but it must be remembered that, good, bad and indifferent, we are viewing the products of a first generation of glass artists working without benefit of a modern tradi-

tion. It is to be expected that much of it will be eclectic. Some will try to stretch the material or technique too far; some, to put it kindly, may not be very competent and may seem pointless; but all of it in one way or another will contribute to the total fund of knowledge and experience from which stem new concepts and criteria. Hopefully, a new idiom will eventually emerge to define more clearly the position and purpose of the studio craftsman.

If experience of the ceramic industry is anything to go by, the industrial craftsman may be somewhat suspicious of the new 'upstarts' and view their efforts as an abuse of material, flouting sound practice. His misgivings may sometimes be justified, but he should try to use discretion and understand the different aims of the studio craftsman. Likewise the latter should not view his industrial counterpart with disdain, as an insensitive operator in an impersonal production process with no interests or abilities beyond those of daily routine. One is complementary to the other and the true craftsman in either sense will acknowledge and value excellence wherever it is to be found.

As for our novice, he might suppose that the achievement of excellence lies in a mysterious amalgam of indeterminate craft skills, years of experience and intuitive sensibilities. But perhaps he can begin to consider himself an artist in glass when he first begins to despair at his own inadequacies.

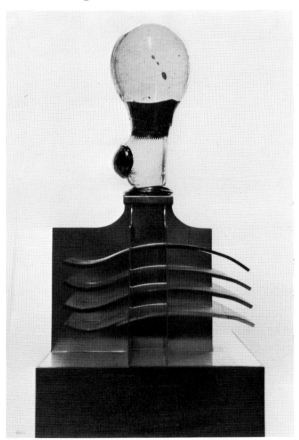

Suppliers of Equipment/ Materials for Small Scale Glassworking

GREAT BRITAIN   U.S.A.

Glassworking Machinery

Glassworks Equipment
Ltd.,
Park Lane,
Halesowen,
Worcs.
(also for
castable refractories)

Lang Machine Works,
156–166 N. May St.,
Chicago,
Ill.

Sommer & Maca Glass
Manufacturing Co.,
5501 West Ogden Ave.,
Chicago,
Ill. 60650

Paoli Clay Co.,
Route 1,
Belleville,
Wisc. 53508

Vacuum Cast Furnace Blocks

Parkinson & Spencer
Ltd.,
Ambler Thorn Fireclay
Works,
Halifax,
Yorks.

Findlay Refractories Co.,
P.O. Box 517,
Washington,
Penna. 15301

Corhart Refractories,
1600 West Lee St.,
Louisville,
Ky. 40210

Castable Refractories

Dyson Monolithics
Group Division,
Diamond Works,
Stoke Old Road,
Hartshill,
Stoke-on-Trent,
ST4 6DP

A. P. Green Firebrick
Corp.,
Mexico,
Missouri 65265

Johns Manville Corp.,
22 East 40th St.,
New York,
N.Y. 10016

Refractories

Gibbons Brierly Hill
Co.,
Brierly Hill,
Staffs.
(also for
castable refractories)

A. P. Green Firebrick
Corp.

Johns Manville Corp.

Babcock & Wilcox
Refractories Division,
Old Savannah Rd.,
Augusta,
Ga. 30903

Burners and Mixers

Keith Blackman Ltd.,
Mill Mead Rd.,
Tottenham Rd.,
London N.17

Stordy Combustion
Engineering Ltd.,
Heath Mill Rd.,
Wombourne,
Wolverhampton,
WV5 8BD

The Aerogen Co.,
Alton,
Hants.

North American Man.
Co.,
4455 East 71st St.,
Cleveland,
Ohio 44105

Eclipse Fuel Eng. Co.,
1100 Buchanan St.,
Rockford,
Ill. 61101

Cullet

Nazeing Glass Works
  Ltd.,
Broxbourne,
Hoddesdon,
Herts.

Johns Manville Corp.,
Glass Fibers Division,
Waterville,
Ohio

Keystone Cullet Co.,
St. Louis and Atlanta,
Georgia

Paoli Clay Co.

Cullet, Coloured Cane and Tube

Plowden & Thompson
  Ltd.,
Dial Glass Works,
Stourbridge,
Worcs.

Epsom Glass Industries,
Longmead Industrial
  Estate,
Epsom,
Surrey
Bishop & Co.,
St. Helens Glass Tube
  Works,
St. Helens,
Lancs.

Blanko Glass Co.,
Milton,
W. Virginia

Corning Glass Works,
Corning,
New York

Chemicals

Griffin & Tatlock,
Kemble St.,
Kingsway,

London W.C.1

Ceramic Colour and
  Chemical Man. Co.
  Inc.,
  Box 297,
New Brighton,
Pa. 15066

The O. Hommel Co.,
Box 475,
Pittsburgh,
Pa. 15230

Colours, Enamels etc.

Blythe Colour Works,
Cresswell,
Stoke-on-Trent,
Staffs.

Harrison Mayer Ltd.,
Meir,
Stoke-on-Trent,
Staffs.

Paoli Clay Co.

Ottawa Silica Co.,
Box 577,
Ottawa,
Ill. 61350

Martin Marietta Corp.,
Manley Sand Division,
Portage,
Wisconsin

Ferro Enamel Co.,
4150 East 56th St.,
Cleveland,
Ohio 44105

Furnaces, Glass Melting Tanks and Glory-Holes

Ferro Ltd.,
Wombourne,
Wolverhampton,
WV5 8PA

Paoli Clay Co.

The Glassworks,
Box 202,
Joppa Rd.,
Warner,
N.H. 03278

Raw Materials for Glass Batchmaking

C. E. Ramsden & Co.
  Ltd.,
Meir,
Stoke-on-Trent,
ST3 7QB

Tongs, Shears, Irons and Accessories

Ferro Ltd.

Paoli Clay Co.

Electric Fans for Furnaces

Buck & Hickman Ltd.,
Whitechapel Rd.,
London E1 1EB

Metal Plate for Marvers

McReady's Metal Co.
  Ltd.,
Paynes Lane,
Rugby,
Warwicks.

Abrasive Materials and Products

The Carborundum Co.
  Ltd.,
P.O. Box 55,
Trafford Park,
Manchester,
M17 1HP

Electric Furnaces, Lehrs, Pyrometers

R. M. Catterson-Smith,
Tollesbury,
Malden,
Essex,
CM9 8SJ

Engraving Machinery

Buck & Hickman Ltd.

Flextol Eng. Co.,
The Green,
Ealing,
London W.5

Sand Blasting Machinery

Buck & Hickman Ltd.

Berlyne Bailey,
29 Smedley Lane,
Cheetham,
Manchester,
M8 86B

Gas-fired Pot Furnaces

Sismey & Linforth,
1631 Coventry Rd.,
Birmingham,
B26 1DD

General Glassmakers' Suppliers

Jencons,
Mark Rd.,
Hemel Hempstead,
Herts.

Index

DATE DUE